Praise for [P9-BJD-183] classic
depiction of the rigors of Marine training
and the terrors of warfare hailed as
"The Red Badge of Courage of the
Vietnam War" *

THE PROUD BASTARDS

"Great stuff! Captures the language, the tedium, the realities of Vietnam."

—Keith William Nolan

"An agonizing, emotional read that merits your attention."

—*The American Veteran* *

"A vividly told account of combat . . . superb reading for anybody wanting to know about life and death in the Vietnam War as seen through the eyes of a combat marine."

—*Midwest Book Review*

"A hard-hitting, blunt memoir."

—*The Veteran*

"This account of the war in Vietnam will hit you like a blow to the kidneys. . . . The power of these words will astound you. Read this book!"

—*Buzz Review News*

THE PROUD BASTARDS

E. Michael Helms

POCKET STAR BOOKS
New York   London   Toronto   Sydney

A Pocket Star Book published by
POCKET BOOKS, a division of Simon & Schuster, Inc.
1230 Avenue of the Americas, New York, NY 10020

Copyright © 1990 by E. Michael Helms

ISBN: 0-7434-8324-3

First Pocket Books printing February 2004

10 9 8 7 6 5 4 3

POCKET STAR BOOKS and colophon are registered trademarks of Simon & Schuster, Inc.

Cover design by Patrick Kang
Cover photo by Catherine Leroy

Manufactured in the United States of America

For information regarding special discounts for bulk purchases, please contact Simon & Schuster Special Sales at 1-800-456-6798 or business@simonandschuster.com.

To Private First Class Guy Robert Bean and
Lance Corporal John Patrick Larkin, and all the others.
Semper Fidelis

*"I have died your deaths a thousand times
as I have grown old. Yet you sleep, forever young
in my memory."*
—E. M. H.

Acknowledgments

Special thanks to:

John Crader, whose tireless efforts and friendship pointed me to the road home;

Jim Bishop, an old soldier of three wars, and a very special friend who always has time for others;

Gregg Brown, Team Leader of the Tallahassee Vet Center, for the many hours spent guiding me back;

Karen, my wife and partner, for all the patience, support, and unconditional love.

To every thing there is a season, and a time to every purpose under the heaven. . . .

—*Ecclesiastes 3:1*

THE PROUD BASTARDS

1

Boot Camp. Parris Island. God, how I had dreamed about that place! Everything I had read and heard about was true. But my romanticized visions of being molded into a United States Marine at the legendary Recruit Training Depot were about to be quickly and rudely transformed into something more closely akin to a nightmare. . . .

Yes, Mikey, there really *is* a Drill Instructor who jumps aboard the bus to welcome your arrival. Only, his maniacal ranting and raving and the most god-awful foul-mouthed ear-bending cursing you never wanted to hear serve to quickly dispel my notion that this is going to even remotely resemble the adventure that I had envisioned. I think I really screwed up this time!

Hey, there really *are* yellow footprints on the pavement for us to line up on as we frantically scramble off the bus at the DI's orders. After being unceremoniously shown how to attain something faintly resembling the military posture of attention, and several of the "herd" being reminded somewhat unkindly that the *other* foot is the left one, we are "marched" to a wooden building and issued field jackets because it is January and it is late at night or early morning and it is very cold. We don the field jackets over our civilian clothing and they become our security blankets, guarding us from the cold outside and somewhat less from the fear-induced lonely chill inside.

We are "herded" (the DI has given up trying to teach such hopeless worthless pieces of shit how to march this night) to another wooden building, a "holding pen" of sorts. It is crammed with metal-framed bunk beds, thin bare mattresses and pillows with neatly folded green woolen blankets at the foot of each. We are ordered to sleep. We try. We fail. We talk very little, but we think very much—confused, disoriented, regretful, self-pitying thoughts: *What have I done? What have I gotten myself into? Oh shit!* is repeated a thousand times in a thousand ways. No one escapes.

Daylight threatens and we are aroused in a surprisingly nonviolent manner by another DI who is not really a DI but at this point we think everyone is a DI. We trudge in mock unison to the shearing room where butchers posing as barbers cause the crowning vestige of our civilian identities to fall in pitiful heaps upon the floor. Blond, black, brunette, red, short, long, curly, straight—nothing matters. We are now all the same.

Another building and we are stripped of our civilian clothes, shoes, belts and all personal effects. We have nothing. We *are* nothing. We are issued olive-drab utility shirts and trousers, web belts and brass buckles, soft covers, black boots, socks and skivvies. We put them on. *Now* we are something: United States Marine Corps recruits— "boots." We are reminded that we are still worthless pieces of shit who will probably never become real Marines, but even that is better than being nothing or being a civilian. We have been promoted.

The sun is getting high in the clear winter sky now and we have been led to a big tin building by an enraged sergeant who we are sure must be one of our bona fide DIs. He is too mean and nasty to be otherwise. It must be catching—everyone is being rude as they "issue" buckets, canteens, mess gear, shelter halves and poles, packs, webbed gear, helmets, punches, pokes, slaps and insults to us. We are soon consoled, however, because we are introduced to our "best friend" who will be with us during our trials and tribulations while on the Island—the M-14 rifle.

We shoulder our burdens and our best friend and double-time toward a large two-story barracks that will be our home until death, desertion, disgrace or graduation do us part.

We are on the second floor of the large white structure and we are standing at attention in front of our racks and we are very scared. Our DIs are introducing themselves to us. Sergeant Bottoms is the DI who escorted us from the tin building. He is young and mean looking and I don't think I like him. Staff Sergeant Burns is slightly paunchy and a sadistical son of a bitch and I'm *sure* I don't like him. Gunnery Sergeant Franz is our Senior Drill Instructor. He is short, built like a cannon ball, and looks somewhat like a bulldog (although most bulldogs I've seen seemed a lot less ferocious than Gunnery Sergeant Franz).

Our Senior DI has just demonstrated that he doesn't take any insolence or other shit off of any maggot recruit—a point-of-fact driven home by the prostrate figure gasping for breath on the squadbay's wooden deck. I am much too intimidated to form a quick opinion of Gunnery Sergeant Franz, as I strongly suspect he can read minds.

We have been instructed as to the proper way to address our Drill Instructors ("Sir, Private so-and-so requests permission to speak to the Drill Instructor, Sir!"); have learned never to refer to ourselves in the first-person ("I"), and never, *never* (Oh Jesus, save my young ass!) refer to our Drill Instructors as "you" ("You? *You?* Are you calling me a 'ewe', Private? With a yard of dick and a sack full of balls, how *dare* you call me a female sheep!").

We have also learned that Marine Corps Drill Instructors are all hard of hearing ("Sir, yes Sir!" I can't hear you. "Sir, yes *Sir!*" I *still* can't hear you, ladies! *"Sir, yes Sir!" Say it like you've got a set, you worthless cunts!* "Sirrr, yesss Sirrr!!!").

We are in a brick building filling out forms according to a corporal's instructions when I see it. The clock on the wall. It is two o'clock in the afternoon of the first day. Oh god, this can't be true! I'm sure I've been here almost forever, and it's only two o'clock? The first day? Maybe I'm dreaming. That's it. We must be filling out some final forms. Soon we'll leave here and march to the parade grounds and pass-in-review and graduate. It can't *still* be the first day—my entire eighteen years haven't lasted this long. But it is. Two o'clock. The first day. Jesus, how time flies when you're having fun.

"Sir, Private Helms requests permission to speak to the Drill Instructor, Sir."

We are back in our barracks and standing at attention in front of our racks (as we must do at all times unless we have been otherwise instructed) and I am feeling sick and I am sure I am going to throw up.

"Speak!"

"Sir, Private Helms requests permission to make a head call, Sir." (We have learned that Marines piss and shit and shave and brush their teeth in the "head," not the bathroom.)

"What's the matter, maggot, fixing to mess your drawers?"

"Sir, no Sir. The private is about to throw up, Sir."

"You *will not* throw up on my beautiful clean deck, will you, Private?"

"Sir, no Sir!"

"Because if you do puke on my beautiful clean deck, you *will* take a spoon and eat it all up, won't you, Private?"

"Sir, yes Sir!"

"And you *will* take a fork and eat up all the chunky pieces, won't you, maggot?"

"Sir, yes Sir!"

"Go!"

"Aye, aye, Sir!"

I double-time down the squadbay and through the hatchway leading to the head. I race to a toilet as waves of salty spit well-up from my throat. I spit into the bowl a few times but don't puke. The nausea subsides. I run back to my rack and assume my statue position.

Time passes. How much time is impossible to ascertain in our bewildered state. We continue to stand frozen before our racks, afraid to commit so much as a twitch lest we incur the wrath of our Drill Instructors. We have been commanded to stand still. We do. A flurry of incoherent thoughts bombards my consciousness: *I am hungry I feel sick I am not really here I am tired I am dreaming I am in a world of shit I do not belong here I think I will tell my Drill Instructor that I have made a mistake and changed my mind and could I please go home now but I don't want to die and that would be suicide this shit can't be real I will wake up soon I can't take this much longer maybe they will let me go home if I just explain that I think I want to change my mind no hard feelings but this isn't quite what I expected the recruiter didn't tell me this shit.*

It is late in the afternoon and we are marching to chow, our first meal on the Island. At least I *think* it is our first meal but I can't be sure because we have been here a long time and we should have eaten before but I don't think we have so this must be our first meal. We "stand at rigid attention—asshole to bellybutton" in single-file waiting to enter the hatchway leading to the mess hall.

In turn we reach the serving counter, execute a left-face, grab a metal tray and lift it smartly upward so that we are staring at our tray as if it were a mirror. We sidestep along the chow line one pace at a time, ever-fighting the temptation to avert our eyes from our muddled reflection toward the myriad sights, sounds and smells our befuddled senses are now starting to detect.

The recruit to my right has dared to remove a hand from his tray to scratch his ear and Staff Sergeant Burns who must have eyes in the back of his head has snatched him out of line and flung him into a table and is proceeding to deride the poor unfortunate's family heritage in a most vile and profane manner. I instantly become self-mesmerized by a tiny speck of dried food clinging to a section of my tray. Up and down the line other miscreants are falling prey to the Drill Instructors' eagle-eyed vision and the mess hall has become a gymnasium as numerous recruits perform various punitive exercises under the guiding berating of a host of DIs. United States Marine Corps Drill Instructors are obviously oblivious to the fact that stress is detrimental to the digestive processes of the human body. But then, we are not human beings, we are mere recruits, boots, maggots, scumbags, lower than whale shit which lies on the bottom of the ocean.

As we reach the servers we lower our trays to receive our chow, being careful to keep our eyes locked straight ahead. The ones serving our chow are also recruits, but they are much different than we are. There is a certain "air" about them. They are "salty." They are in the last stages of their training. Their metamorphosis is nearly complete. They will soon be real Marines. We feel like shit before their eyes and they know it and they love it. The bastards.

We proceed to our tables where we are commanded to sit in unison, bow our heads in unison and pray in unison. Fi-

nally, Gunnery Sergeant Franz barks the long-awaited order:
"Eat!"

With relish I gaze hungrily at the contents of my heavily
laden tray. Oh, god! Liver and onions floating in a milky
gravy. I think I am going to be sick again. I can't possibly eat
this shit! But I do, because I have been ordered to. I just
hope I don't have to eat it again later, off the squadbay
deck. . . .

> *Dear Mama,*
> *I have arrived here at Parris Island, and it's just*
> *about what I expected. They treat us pretty rough,*
> *but it's all for our own good. I'll just have to stick it*
> *out and do my best.*
> *It has been the longest day that I can remember.*
> *It seemed like at least three weeks.*
> *You ought to see my hair! I look like Yul Bryn-*
> *ner! I've met a few guys and am getting along fine.*
> *How is everybody doing? I hope y'all are doing*
> *fine. I don't have much time but my return address*
> *is on the envelope. Tell everybody to write soon.*
> *Love, Mike*

I have hurriedly scribbled down this letter during
what's left of our "free time." We are graciously allotted
thirty minutes each night to sit on our inverted buckets
and write home to family or friends. Of course, before we
can attend to such correspondence, we must first shit
shower shave brush our teeth scrub our web belts and soft
covers shine our brass buckles polish our boots and—
most importantly—clean and oil our best friend M-14

rifle. Then we can lounge upon our buckets and write to our heart's content.

I really like the stationery. The Marine Corps has graciously provided us worthless shitbirds with matching writing paper and envelopes with the Iwo Jima flag-raising emblazoned on them. Despite the shock and rigors of the past hours, a faint glimmer of esprit de corps stirs somewhere deep within our gut as we gaze upon the immortalized image of real Marines from long ago. Maybe, just maybe, there is hope for us yet.

"Prepare to mount!"

Oh, shit! Staff Sergeant Burns and Sergeant Bottoms have come to tuck us in. We stand before our racks and "count off." There are seventy-seven lowly maggot recruits on deck.

"Mount!"

One hundred fifty-four elbows and seventy-seven assholes swing madly into motion, scrambling frantically into seventy-seven racks and lie frozen at attention.

"Get out of them goddamn racks you goddamn shit maggots you're too goddamn slow!"

One hundred fifty-four elbows and seventy-seven assholes levitate to instant attention before their racks.

"Mount!"

Another frenetic dive to our racks.

Another tirade of blasphemous oaths as Sergeant Bottoms this time beckons us to exit our racks.

After five or six tries we must have gotten it right, or maybe they have just given up on trying to teach us hopeless ones the proper manner of retiring for the night. At any rate, we have just finished singing the

"Marine's Hymn" and the Lord's Prayer, still lying at attention.

"Goodnight, ladies!"

"Sir, goodnight, Sir!"

"I can't *hearrr youuu!*"

"Sirrr, goodnight, Sirrr!!!"

"Sleep!"

Exhaustion prevails, mercifully ending the long day.

2

Lights are flashing on and off, on and off, and muffled shouts pervade my dream. It is so pleasant to be snuggled in my bed against the night's chill, and I am in that wonderful state of being just awake enough to realize how good it will feel to sink back into deep slumber. If those voices and lights will cease now, thank you, I will get on with my sleep.

I am suddenly falling in my dream, but that is okay because I have fallen many times before in my dreams but I never hit the ground because they say if you fall in your dream and hit the ground you will die but I always wake up first.

Oh god! I just landed very hard on my side on the ground, only it is not the ground but a wooden floor I feel beneath my shaken body. I am not dead but I think I wish I was as my eyes open to behold a horrible ogre in a Smokey-the-Bear hat staring down at me with murder in his eyes. Oh shit. Staff Sergeant Burns. Boot Camp.

"Get your goddamn scudsy ass off that deck you worthless shitmaggot!" (Staff Sergeant Burns has such a way with words!)

I fight from under the mattress and covers which accompanied me on my sky dive from the top berth and hurriedly come to attention before my rack which is now leaning at an odd angle against the rack next to it which is leaning against the next rack which is . . .

The squadbay is in shambles. Mattresses, pillows, blankets, foot lockers, and buckets lay in disarray among overturned and tilting racks. All three of our DIs are in a rabid rage as they curse and scream and threaten and hurl garbage cans and shocked recruits down the center aisle.

"You worthless motherfuckers think you can sleep all goddamn day, don't you?"

"Sir, *no* Sir!"

"Listen up, maggots. This is *my* Marine Corps, not your fucking mommy's house, and you will sleep when *I* say sleep, and you will damn well get up when *I* say get up. Is that clear?"

"Sir, yes Sir!"

"I can't *hearrr youuu!*"

"*Sir, yes sirrr!!!*"

"Sergeant Burns, Sergeant Bottoms, come here quickly!" says Gunnery Sergeant Franz, who is standing in front of a red-faced recruit with a bladder-induced erection protruding from the front opening of his skivvy drawers.

"We've got a goddamn faggot-maggot in our midst!"

Burns and Bottoms are on either side of the hapless recruit, their ugly faces inches from the private's own scarlet profile. Gunnery Sergeant Franz maintains his frontal attack, his eyes glancing alternately from the recruit's terror-stricken face to the source of his embarrassment and back again.

"I do believe this private is queer for my gear, don't you, Sergeant Burns?"

"Sure looks that way, Gunny."

"How about it, Private, you wanna butt-fuck your Senior Drill Instructor?"

"Sir, no Sir."

"Then what-the-fuck is that one-eyed skivvy snake poking his puny head out of your drawers for, maggot?"

"Sir, the private doesn't know, Sir."

The poor recruit's color has changed from deep red to pale white and tears have begun to creep down his freckled cheeks.

"Oh, so you don't like me, do you, Private?" snarls Gunnery Sergeant Franz.

"Sir, yes Sir!"

"So! You *are* queer for me!"

"Sir, no Sir!"

"Then you hate me, don't you, Private?"

"Sir, no Sir!"

"Well, make up your mind! Do you love me, Private?"

"Sir, yes Sir!"

"Oh, so you *do* want to butt-fuck me, don't you, maggot?"

"Sir, yes . . . no . . . Sir, the private is confused, Sir."

"Sergeant Burns, what are we going to do with this faggot-maggot and his skivvy snake?"

"I guess we better kill it before it tries to crawl up somebody's ass, Gunny."

"Let's smash it to death," offers Sergeant Bottoms.

"Good idea, Sergeant."

"Hit the deck, fairy!"

The recruit slams belly-first onto the squadbay's hard wooden deck.

"Get up! Get up!"

"Hit it!"

Down he goes again with a sickening thud.

"Get up, goddamn it, get up you're too fucking slow!"

He struggles to his feet.

"Hit it!"

Another belly-buster.

"Reckon it's dead yet, Gunny?"

"Looks like it is, Sergeant. Either dead or unconscious."

Franz grabs the stunned recruit by the throat. "You fairy motherfucker, you keep that pitiful little worm inside your drawers or I'll cut the son of a bitch off the next time. *Is that clear, faggot?"*

"Sir, yes Sir!" answers the bruised recruit, tears now flowing freely down his face.

God, I sure hope it's true about them putting saltpeter in our chow. . . .

It is midmorning and we have marched to a group of buildings where we are going to undergo our physical examinations. We are led into a long corridor and are told to strip to the waist by a tall skinny man in a blue sailor suit. We hang our skivvy shirts and utility jackets on numbered hooks and proceed single-file into a brightly lit room with cold white walls.

Jesus! On either side of a narrow aisle stand several evil-grinning hospital corpsmen armed with pistol-like pneumatic hypodermic weapons clenched in their fists. Gunnery Sergeant Franz, with hands on hips and an evil smirk on his bulldog kisser, stands at the far end as an encouragement for us not to flinch as we enter the gauntlet like cattle going to slaughter.

Now, I have never been one to be afraid of getting a shot, but this shit is a little much. *Pow! Pow!* Those damn things sound like air hammers at a construction site. Oh, shit. Both arms at once. Don't flinch—Gunnery Sergeant Franz is just waiting for somebody to screw up, and it ain't gonna be me. Damn, those things *hurt.* It feels like the needles are meeting somewhere near mid-thorax.

After about a dozen spearings of each arm, we move into a spacious room void of any furnishings. There are two yellow lines painted on the concrete deck and we stand in two columns on these lines facing each other across the room. We are told to strip naked. We place our remaining clothing in neat piles behind us, and again face each other. Weak smiles of embarrassment and a tinge of crimson appear on several faces. The smiles are quickly removed at the behest of our omnipresent Senior Drill Instructor. The color, in varying shades, remains.

Gunnery Sergeant Franz finds the unfortunate recruit with the hapless hard-on from this morning's episode and informs him in no uncertain terms that he had better not start drooling at the sight of all the swinging dicks in the room (although most are nowhere near swinging from the combination of fear and embarrassment). Four more corpsmen appear in the room. Two of them are pushing carts with several boxes of various sizes on them. Another of the corpsmen informs us that we are first going to have a "short

arm" inspection. At his command we are to reach down with
our right hand and peel back the foreskin from our penis, if
we are not circumcised. If we have been circumcised, we are
to stand there with our peter in our palm anyway.

"Do it!"

Seventy-seven right hands grab seventy-seven penises
and stretch them out and peel them back. Jesus, this is em-
barrassing, standing at attention with my dick in my hand!

The corpsmen make their way up and down the
columns, stopping occasionally to lecture a recruit on
the importance of proper hygiene, or to let one know
that he must belong on the other side of the Island with
the women recruits from the looks of that "ridiculous
thing." Gunnery Sergeant Franz warns the corpsmen to
beware of the faggot-maggot and not turn their backs to
him or they might get a pecker up their posterior.

"Jesus H. Christ—what is *this!*"

Gunnery Sergeant Franz and the other corpsmen rush
over to where one of the pecker-checkers has found a
black recruit with what looks like a thick coating of cream
cheese covering the head of his penis.

"Goddamn, maggot! Didn't your mama ever teach you
how to *bathe?*" screams our enraged Senior DI. "Don't
they have soap where you come from, boy?"

"Sir, yes Sir!"

"You ever had contact with a bar of it, boy?"

"Sir, yes Sir!"

The corpsmen have joined in the verbal battering of the
pathetic private, relentlessly pelting him from all sides with
every conceivable four-letter word, phrase and oath they
can muster. Gunnery Sergeant Franz grabs him by the back

of the neck and flings him to the unyielding concrete deck with a resounding slap. He places a spit-polished boot on the quivering recruit's neck.

"Get this filthy scumbag out of my sight and wash that goddamn cheese off that black worm before I stomp his goddamn worthless guts out!"

The trembling recruit, now a strange ashen-gray color, is led away by one of the corpsmen to learn a lesson in personal hygiene. We shudder at the thought.

We have been ordered to lean over and grab our ankles. The corpsmen are making their way behind the columns checking our rectums. Jesus, what a job they've got, shoving their fingers up dozens of assholes every day. They seem to be moving awfully fast—I sure hope they're changing those rubber gloves after each stop. God, I haven't shit in three days. I hope nothing weird happens. Oh, christ. It feels like he's shoving his whole damn forearm up my ass! Damn, he must have big fingers.

I am standing shoulder-to-shoulder with five other recruits before a urinal trough trying my damndest to piss in a specimen bottle. The guys directly beside me have changed twice already. I know the ones lined up behind me must be getting a little impatient. If I don't hurry up Gunnery Sergeant Franz will notice my line isn't moving and I'm going to catch hell and that thought sure doesn't help because now I don't think I have to pee even worse than before!

Maybe I can get one of the guys beside me to give me a little of his, but I better not risk asking because that maniac is bound to catch me talking and then I'd probably wind up in the trough.

I'll close my eyes and pretend I'm home alone in the
bathroom and the door is closed and locked and nobody is
around and boy I really have to go bad and won't it feel good
to finally pee and—*shit!* I can't pretend good enough and
the guys on both sides of me have changed again. I concentrate all my efforts and strain really hard—I'm grunting I'm
straining so hard. My face must be red as a beet. Ah,
yeahhh. Finally. It's not much, but I sure as hell hope it's
enough, as hard as that stuff was to come by. . . .

Dear Mama,

    *It's my second day here and I'm so confused I
don't even know what day it is. It's getting rougher
all the time, but so far it's been fair.*

    *I'm so tired that I can hardly keep my eyes open,
but don't worry about me. When I get home I'm
going to stretch out on the couch and not move for
twenty days. . . .*

    *I sure am homesick. It seems like I've been gone
a year.*

    *We got our physicals today, and the shots really
hurt now. I'm pooped! You wouldn't believe how
tough it is up here.*

    *How is everybody? Say hello to everybody and tell
them to write soon. Don't send any packages, though.*

    Love, Mike

Free time over . . . Count off . . . Seventy-seven recruits
on deck, Sir! Prepare to mount . . . Mount . . . Sing . . .
Pray . . . Goodnight, ladies . . . Sir, goodnight, Sir!
Sleep . . . Thank god.

3

The bright beam from the flashlight I carry allows me to read the time from the clock above the squadbay hatchway. It is 2400 hours—midnight—and it is Saturday night. Or is it Sunday morning? Oh well, it doesn't really matter, considering where I'm at.

I'm beginning my second hour of "fire watch" duty. Each night four lucky recruits spend two hours apiece patrolling the squadbay, head and hallway of our platoon area. We make sure that all recruits stay neatly tucked in their racks (lest some crazed idiot be foolish enough to attempt to go "over the hill"), see that no intruders invade our sacred platoon area, and of course (as befits the name) act as an early-warning device should these vintage World War Two–era barracks decide to burn down around us. We are to report any violation or unusual occurrence to the Duty Drill Instructor. Nothing out of the ordinary hardly ever happens, thank god, because who in the hell would want to wake up a sleeping monster?

I complete another tour down the length of the long

squadbay, making sure I don't shine the light directly in anyone's eyes as I check to see if all the poor bastards are still here. They are. Shit, you'd really have to be crazy to try and escape from this asylum. First of all, the Island is just that—a real island, connected to the real world only by a heavily guarded causeway. Which leaves the prospective escapee a choice of dying, swimming or staying. If you die during training they'll box you up and ship you home—no problem there. If you try swimming you're going to die anyway, what with the treacherous currents, man-eating sharks, alligators and Drill Instructors surrounding the Island. That leaves staying. Not necessarily an easy choice, but the one of preference, nonetheless.

Saturday night. Man, if I was home right now me and my friends would be at the beach at the Hang Out trying to pick up girls. No you wouldn't, stupid. It's the middle of winter and the beach is deserted and the Hang Out is closed. Okay, I'd be cruising Panama City, down Harrison Avenue around the marina, then down Sixth Street and around Jimmy's Drive-In trying to pick up girls. Yeah. And we'd stop at Jimmy's and I'd order me one of those world-famous gigantic dinner-plate-size hamburgers and a large order of french fries and onion rings smothered in ketchup and a large cherry Coke or maybe a chicken box or maybe a shrimp box or maybe all of it. . . . Damn, I'm hungry. I can't seem to get enough to eat up here. There's always plenty of chow piled on my tray, but I'm still almost always hungry. I even ate my Chapstick the other night during free-time, and that's no bullshit. Must be all the exercise we're getting. There sure as hell is no shortage of that.

Saturday night. Damn. I'm homesick. I've been here for five days now, I think. Wow, only nine and a half more *weeks* to go. Might as well be years. This shit will never end. I'll be here for*ever*. Maybe we're all dead and this is really Hell and I'm here because of the wonderful life I led. Could be. This sure ain't Heaven, and those DIs *are* mean devils. Hey, that's kinda funny. I stifle a small chuckle.

Only five days. I wish I was home. Why the hell did I ever do a crazy thing like join the Marine Corps, anyway? I pass the light over the cold tile environ of the head. No privates seeking midnight relief. Sleep is too valuable a commodity here.

I slip quietly through the hatchway into the hallway, scanning the beam over the area. Equipment locker is secure. The DI's office is secure. Through the closed hatch of the Duty Drill Instructor's sleeping quarters I hear heavy snoring. Sounds like a goddamn grizzly. Must be Burns. Yeah, it's Burns. I remember the son of a bitch tucking us in after about five thousand push-ups just to harass our young asses:

"Goodnight, pussies."

"Sir, goodnight, Sir!" (Yeah, goodnight you sorry motherfucker. I hope you fucking die in your sleep.)

God, I wish I was out of this place. How did I ever get myself in this shit? You joined, stupid. Real smart move, Mikey. Well, there's nothing I can do about it now. Only five days. Seems like years since I rode that Greyhound to the Montgomery Induction Center with Cantrell and McKeithen. Only one more hour and we'd be on a plane bound for Charleston, and then that First Sergeant comes walking up all somber-looking and asks which one of us is Helms, and I say "I am, Sir," and he says "I'm sorry son, but your father just died," and then I'm on another bus headed back home again and my buddies are off to Parris Island and I've got to go into that house and watch everybody cry and carry on and a week later I'm back in Montgomery alone heading for this place. Oh well, such is life.

I look at the clock again. It is now 2430 hours, or is that 0030 hours? No, it's 2430. Thirty more minutes and then I can wake up my relief and then I can sleep. Boy, am I tired. They have really had us hopping the last few days. Aptitude tests and close-order drill and interviews and more tests and close-order drill and lectures and close-order drill and physical fitness and close-order drill and learning our Eleven General Orders and close-order drill and learning our chain of command and close-order drill and learning guard duty movements and procedures and close-order drill and disassembly and assembly of our best friend M-14 rifle and close-order drill and close-order drill and close-order drill.

Man, we've done so much close-order drill and manual-of-arms that I think we could do it in our sleep. It must be paying off, though. Our platoon is really shaping up. We're going to be the best platoon in our series—maybe even on the whole damn Island.

It's 0100 hours. Finally. Time to wake up the next fire-watch. I gently shake and whisper him awake. When he is dressed I pass him the flashlight and white helmet-liner the firewatch wears. I undress and slip beneath the warm woolen blanket and clean sheets of my rack. I have five beautiful hours to sleep because tomorrow—or rather, today—is Sunday, and reveille is an hour later than usual.

I close my eyes, and one more day is behind me. . . .

> *Tuesday, January 31, 1967*
>
> *Dear Mama,*
>
> *Well, I've been here for a week now and am pretty well adjusted to the routine of our barrack's life here. I sure miss home and can't wait to get back. Military life isn't really bad except it is boring and you don't have enough time to do anything and you're constantly being screamed at, etc. The days are growing shorter it seems, and the routine is getting more clear. I've been sort of sick since I got here, but now I'm beginning to feel better. I think it was the flu or a cold. My appetite has really picked up. At first I thought the food was terrible, but now it seems to be real good. But I've been constipated since I left home.*
>
> *What's happening on the local and national scenes? I heard something about some astronauts. What happened?*
>
> *We had to do a lot of punishment exercises today because a lot of people were goofing off. That's pretty rough. I didn't get a letter tonight. I sure wish y'all would write more often. Letters and chow are all I have to look forward to these days.*
>
> *Say hello to everyone for me.*
>
> *Love, Mike*

4

I am standing beside the hatchway of our Drill Instructors' office and I am in a true world of shit. I finally screwed up, and how! This evening at chow I got caught talking in the chow line with Dan Coker, a buddy of mine from South Carolina, and now we are going to pay for it but good. It was just a quick whispered exchange about how hungry we both always are, but ol' Eagle-ears Burns heard us. I swear, that bastard could hear a gnat fart in a tornado. And of course, with *my* luck it had to be Burns who has the duty tonight. If it was Sergeant Bottoms or even Gunnery Sergeant Franz we might have a slight chance of surviving what's coming, but with Attila the Hun pulling the strings the situation is definitely in doubt. Oh well, no sense putting off the inevitable.

We stand at attention with our left shoulders next to the bulkhead just before the closed hatch wherein waits the monster. In true recruit-reporting form I raise my right arm high above my head and sharply strike the bulkhead three times with my open palm. . . . No response. A faint glimmer of hope cautiously stirs within me. Maybe he's forgotten he told us to report and he's busy elsewhere during our free time or maybe he had a heart attack and died or . . .

Coker swallows nervously behind me. I knock again.

"Who's that woodpecker pecking at my hatch?"

Shit! He's here and still alive.

"Sir, Private Helms reporting to the Drill Instructor as ordered, Sir!"

"Sir, Private Coker reporting to the Drill Instructor as ordered, Sir!" parrots Coker.

"Enter!"

We march into the lion's den, execute a smart left-face and snap to rigid attention before the desk. Burns puts down his paperwork and sneers at us from his swivel chair.

"So, you peckerheads think you can wag your raggedy-ass tongues in my chow line, do you?"

"Sir, no Sir!" we shout in duet.

"What's so goddamn important that you two maggots had to disrupt my chow time for?"

"Sir, the privates were talking about how hungry they were, Sir," I volunteer, rather weakly.

"Hungry? *Hungry?* You shitheads only eat for one reason, and that's to resupply your worthless asses with more energy, is that right privates?"

"Sir, yes Sir!"

"Well, if you've got enough energy left to grab-ass in my chow line, then you must not be getting enough exercise, right privates?" An evil leer gleams from his beady eyes now.

"Sir, yes Sir!" Oh shit, here we go.

Burns leads us into the hallway to the equipment locker. He takes out two bottles of ammonia and hands one to each of us. We are instructed to stand on opposite ends of the hallway and to pour the ammonia onto the wooden deck at our feet.

We do. The puddles spread quickly around us, and the sharp vapors instantly permeate our eyes, nose and mouth.

"Bends and thrusts, privates. Two hundred of them. And since you shitbirds like to talk so much, you *will* count-off every one of them. *Is that clear!*"

"Sir, yes Sir!"

"Begin!"

"One-two-three, *one Sir!* One-two-three, *two Sir!* One-two-three, *three Sir!*"

Ah, bends and thrusts. A most effective four-count exercise. Count "one" and bend your knees and come to a squatting position with palms flat on the deck. Count "two" and thrust your legs out behind you and assume a push-up position. Count "three" and quickly pull both legs back under you, again assuming a squatting position. Count "four" and spring back to attention at the original standing position. Add a puddle of ammonia and you truly have a most delightful way to spend one's free time!

Damn, this ammonia has really got my attention. The coaches used to use this shit on us when we'd get knocked groggy playing football. This much would wake up the dead. I can't breathe, shit, but I can't stop and I've got to keep counting. My face and neck and eyes and throat are burning like hell. God, I'm gonna *die*. I can barely see now for all the tears but I can't wipe my eyes because the shit is all over my hands and my sleeves are soaked. Jesus, I can't *breathe*. Shit . . . don't panic . . . think!

After about thirty or forty repetitions I finally figure out that if I inhale after shouting "Sir" at the end of each count with my head tilted back, I can gulp enough air to survive this ordeal. My panic has turned to anger and my thoughts zero in on my hatred for Burns. If I ever get just half a chance I'm gonna kill that son of a bitch. Motherfucker. My dreams of revenge keep me going.

We are somewhere near half-way through our second hundred when Burns stops us and orders us to hit the showers. Do I detect a hint of humanity in the heinous bastard? Hell no. He probably just couldn't come up with a reasonable explanation as to how two recruits died of ammonia poisoning.

Another haircut this morning. That's our second one in two weeks—definitely a record for me. Just when I had enough to almost pinch—*zip*. No heaps of hair cascading to the deck this time; just a sprinkling of minute bristles dusting around our shoulders. Sandpaper scalp once again.

Back to the dispensary for more shots. Damn, just when the soreness from the first barrage was starting to subside. *Ouch*. Hey, not too bad. Only four this time.

They've given us a small paper cup with a funny-looking pill in it. They tell us it's for "cat fever" (whatever the hell that is). The corpsman says it is not mandatory that we take the pill, but if we catch the fever we will be set back a week in training. No further encouragement to partake is needed.

Time seems to be passing rather quickly now. The shock and confusion of the first few days has eased, and we stay so busy with classes and lectures and training films and drilling that the sun no longer appears to stand still.

Tonight in our squadbay Gunnery Sergeant Franz set up a projector and we watched a film of actual combat footage of Marines in Vietnam. One sequence showed some Marines on patrol when one tripped a booby-trap wounding several men. Another showed a Marine throwing a hand grenade into a bunker and then two more Marines rushing up and firing their rifles into the bunker after the explosion. But everybody's favorite part of the film was when a Marine platoon received fire from a tree line on their flank. They turned and got on-line, and charged through the ambush, firing their weapons and hurling grenades and epithets at the retreating VC. God, that was exciting. We all cheered and screamed encouragement and wished like hell that we were there with them. Most of us soon will be. Our Senior DI told us that within three or four months probably ninety percent of us will be in Vietnam as grunts. Man, I can't wait. That's what I joined the Marines for—to fight.

Gunnery Sergeant Franz also informed us that his own orders for Vietnam have come through, and that he will be leaving us in a few weeks. He said he thought we were going to make damn fine Marines, and that he would be proud to serve with us over there. Damn, the bastard almost made us start crying from pride and esprit de corps. He's not too bad after all. Of course, that means we'll be getting another DI to take his place. Christ, I sure as hell hope that Burns doesn't take over as Senior DI. That would be too fucking much. Maybe the gods will have mercy on us and send us a new Senior Drill Instructor instead of promoting Burns. I sure as shit hope so. . . .

Tuesday, February 14, 1967
    Dear Mama,
    Today marks my third week here. But I still have six or seven more to go, so they say. I didn't even realize it was Valentine's Day until I got the valentines. Thanks a lot. I wish I had one to send to y'all, but I guess y'all understand that that's not possible.
    A guy got some valentine candy from his mother tonight. We could have a piece if we would do one hundred bends and thrusts, and that's a hard exercise to do. As hungry as I am, I didn't take one, but some fools did.
    Did I tell you that I've gained six pounds already? Well, I have. Tonight for chow we had T-bone steaks!
    Yesterday we started hand-to-hand combat. We learned how to fall properly. Today we learned one of our throwing movements. Nobody better try picking on me when I get home. I'm the meanest Marine alive! Ha! Ha!
    The pocket calendar is perfect. Now I can mark off the days until I leave this hell-hole. And thanks for the stamps, too.
    I've gotta go again. Thanks for everything, and tell everybody I said hello and to write.
    Love, Mike

5

We are inside the regimental gymnasium for another class of hand-to-hand-combat training. The cold, steel-gray girders of the huge structure reflect the bitterness of the late South Carolina winter afternoon. We are thankful for the temporary respite from the endless marching and drilling on the arctic-blasted parade deck.

In past lessons we have learned the proper way to protect ourselves when taking a fall, and have walked through our basic throwing movements. We have also learned several vital areas of the human body which we can exploit in our attack upon our enemy. We can break our enemy's nose with a sharp chopping blow of our hand and then dispatch him by using our palm to drive the fractured bone into his brain's frontal lobe. We can also cause his demise with a quick vicious jab to the throat, crushing or severing his windpipe. Or, we can render our enemy helpless by jamming our fingers deep into his sockets and ripping out his eyeballs. All of these offensive tactics can be made easier and more effective if we first "soften-up" our enemy with a crushing blow of our fist to his groin. We all agree with the instructor that such a blow would definitely dampen one's defenses!

Today we are to practice our attacks and throws at full speed, although we are to stop short of actually breaking noses, piercing brains, crushing windpipes, plucking eyeballs, bashing balls, etc. We remove our boots and pair off into two opposing teams on the padded tumbling mat which covers most of the huge gymnasium deck.

My "enemy" is Private Finley. Private Finley is a shitbird. Although our DIs call all of us "shitbird" now and then, Private Finley is a genuine shitbird. A true fuck-up. A ten-percenter. A non-hacker. Several times a week he causes the entire platoon to endure punishment PT because of his slacker attitude. A chain is only as strong as its weakest link—our DIs have drilled this fact into us time and time again, thanks to Private Finley. His type will get us killed in combat, we are told.

Yet, Private Finley does not seem to care or try to improve. He simply goes through the motions, doing just enough to barely scrape by. He seems to be void of esprit de corps. He whines and complains and makes excuses. We do exercises because of Private Finley. Many, many repetitions. We run around the parade grounds for Private Finley. Many, many laps. Private Finley goes to sickbay almost every morning at sick call. Our Drill Instructors are very displeased with Private Finley, but they keep taking their frustrations out on the entire platoon. We think our Drill Instructors are trying to teach us something.

Private Finley's team is to ward off my team's half-speed attack first. A whistle sounds and I advance toward Private Finley and throw a right hand at his head. He barely manages to block my mock blow, grabs my utility shirt, turns and weakly throws me over his hip. I scream *"Die!,"* expelling the air from my lungs and sharply slap the deck with my left arm to absorb the force of the fall as we have been instructed. Finley's limp hand falls across the bridge of my nose in a "killing" blow. He leans down to my face and whispers, "Hey, let's take it easy on each other, okay?"

Private Finley disgusts me. Why didn't this pussy join the Air Force or the Girl Scouts? How in the hell did he ever get into the Marines? I have suffered enough for this shitbird! I have no intentions of catching hell from the instructor or our DIs which is exactly what will happen if they see that we are slacking it.

It is my turn. The whistle sounds. Private Finley ambles forward with a growl that resembles a purring cat. I block his half-hearted swing with my left forearm, step quickly placing my right foot between his spread stance, and jam my fist into his soft, flabby belly.

"Oomphh!" The breath rushes from Finley's lungs and his eyes open wide in shocked surprise. I grab his utility shirt, thrust my right hip high into his midsection, pivot quickly and fling him over my side. He hits the mat with a heavy thud.

Private Finley does not get up when the command is given. He flounces around on the mat and acts like he is dying, crying and clutching his shoulder and trying to catch his breath. He is a pitiful sight but we are not sorry for him. It is his own fault. Private Finley has fucked-up once again. He has not learned how to fall properly. He has paid for his own slackness this time.

We are back in our squadbay and are preparing to march to evening chow. Private Finley has requested permission to go to sickbay to have his shoulder examined. He is sure it is broken. We are sure he is faking, but we hope he is not. If he is really hurt he will be taken out of our platoon while he recuperates and set back in training with a new platoon.

I feel good inside. The platoon feels good. We have become One. There is no room for shitbird slackers in Two Forty-two, for we are the best platoon on the Island.

Bayonet training. How to rip, slash, stab, gut, smash, butt and crush your enemy to death in several simple lessons. We have been taught that Marine Corps bayonet fighting movements are similar to those employed by boxers, and that aggressiveness is the key element. We are green-clad Rocky Marcianos with sabre-tipped M-14 rifles in our hands. We will close with our enemy, strike fear in his heart and soul with a bloodcurdling scream, and then attack with a ferocity and vengeance from which there is no possible escape. We will cause his guts to spill from his belly. We will bash his brains from his skull. We will totally annihilate him and then jump on his chest and do a war dance and stomp his worthless heart out and then leave his filthy carcass for the vultures to devour. We are lean and mean killing machines.

In days past we have "destroyed" dozens of enemy dummies with a flurry of jabs, slashes, horizontal and vertical butt-strokes and smashes. We have fended off our attackers by using our rifles like the shields of ancient warriors, parrying left and right, but always following up these defensive measures with an assault that would cause the Spartans of old to gaze down upon us with a knowing nod and an approving smile.

Today we are going to use our newly acquired killing skills and techniques on a real, live enemy—Platoon Two Forty from our series. We hate the bastards and they hate us. They think they are the biggest, baddest platoon on the Island. They are full of shit. Earlier this week we blew them and the other platoons away in our Series Drill Competition. The plaque on the Bronzed Boot awarded the winners reads *Platoon Two Forty-two*.

They have tried to break our ranks in the chow line several times and we have mixed it up pretty good. The Drill Instructors from both platoons seem to go out of their way to create situations that will pit their recruits against each other like illegal fighting dogs. And now we are going to go at it with bayonets.

Well, not exactly. The DIs are smart enough to realize that they have trained us well and have created such loyalty in us that we really *would* try to kill each other with bayonets if so ordered. We will make battle with pugil sticks.

Each fighting recruit is fitted with a masked football helmet, padded hockey gloves and armored jock strap. We look like a weekend warrior who can't decide whether he belongs on the gridiron or the ice. Our "weapon" is a five-foot-long stick with heavy padding on either end substituting for razor-honed bayonets and hardwood stocks.

Our platoon is faring rather well. We are winning more than we are losing. The bayonet instructors are the judges. They stop the matches with a shrill blast from their whistles when they determine a "killing blow" to a vital area has been struck. The Drill Instructors act as coaches, alternately praising or razing their charges, depending on the outcome and performances of the individual battles.

I am next. I will do well. I must. I will close with my enemy and destroy him! I look across the field of battle to size up my foe. About the same height, maybe a little heavier. Be aggressive. Be quick.

The whistle sounds. We charge, our war cries drowning out the cheers and shouts of encouragement from our respective platoons. We crash together with simultaneous horizontal butt strokes, both missing their mark. I jab at his throat; he parries and follows with a slash which I block. I combine a hard slash with a vicious vertical butt stroke designed to make him a eunuch, but he parries the first and sidesteps the second.

We circle around and around, each looking for an opening to drive home a fatal blow. Our platoons cheer us on and our DIs threaten us to further action. Damn, my enemy is good—a hell of a lot faster than I thought he would be. Where the hell is Finley when I need him?

Jab—parry. Slash—parry. With another scream I fake a slash and quickly thrust a jab toward his chest. At the last possible instant he recovers from my feint and barely manages to avoid my jab with a desperate block. He counters instantly with a violent slash aimed at my exposed neck, a well-executed maneuver that has caught me momentarily off-balance. It is all I can do to lift my "rifle" and partially block his move, his "bayonet" striking a glancing blow to my right shoulder. The death-whistle sounds, declaring my opponent the winner. I instantly jump to attention before the instructor.

"Sir, the private was only hit in the shoulder, Sir!"

The judge is duly unimpressed with my objection. A huge meaty fist grabs my facemask and flings me to the ground like a practice dummy.

"You are one dead motherfucker, and dead motherfuckers cannot speak—*is that clear, maggot?*"

"Sir, yes Sir!" I rise from the dead and sprint to the end of my platoon's line to await my redemption. I am mad. I am really pissed. I fought well and got cheated. I'll show that bastard next time.

I am psyched up. My adrenalin is really pumping. I charge with a bellow that would do King Kong justice. We circle. He throws a horizontal butt stroke toward my head. His blow strikes only air as I duck, and from the crouch thrust a mighty jab at his throat with everything I have. My "bayonet" catches him fully under the chin and lifts him completely off his feet. He falls flat on his back and I am on him before he can even begin to recover. The death knell has sounded but I have tasted my enemy's blood and I cannot stop. He is *mine!* I hammer blow after blow upon his helmet. I am an uncaged, enraged animal. I want to see his brains flow from his crushed skull. I want to tear his heart out and eat it. His chest is my footstool—*Kill! Kill! Kill!*.

"Goddamn good kill, Private!"

Gunnery Sergeant Franz's voice snaps me back to

reality. I back away from my conquered and still-prone opponent. Gunnery Sergeant Franz turns toward our platoon.

"Now *that's* the way you kill the goddamn enemy!"

Our platoon erupts into screams and cheers. I trot back to the rear of the platoon amid back slaps and "way to go's!" I have hit the grandslam home run and won the game before the home town crowd. I am floating on Cloud Nine. Even our Senior Drill Instructor has praised me.

I am elated, but there is something else. Somewhere, deep within the inner recesses of my mind, the question has been answered. I can kill. . . .

Friday, February 24, 1967

Dear Mama,

This has been a pretty eventful week so far. We had our Series Drill Competition. Of course, Two Forty-two won first place! For this we received a bronzed boot on a plaque for the platoon. Our Drill Instructors were happy over this and gave us permission to undo our top shirt button. That is a pretty big thing up here. We now get to compete in the Regimental Drill Competition, but I don't know when that is yet.

We've had a lot of hand-to-hand combat and bayonet fighting. I did real well in both of these. My chances of making PFC are looking good, I think.

Monday part of our platoon was taken to the infirmary where we "voluntarily" gave blood for

Vietnam. After they took out about ten gallons they
gave us a Coca-Cola, so it was well worth it. I probably won't get another one until I graduate. Also
Monday we got a fifteen-dollar paycheck, but they
made us buy a whole bunch of crap they said we
needed with it, so now I have about two dollars left.
Oh well, that's life. I never could hang on to money
anyway.

Today we ran the Confidence Course. It was real
scary. On number six you climbed a rope and then a
big ladder with the rungs about five feet apart until
you were fifty-five feet above the ground with nothing under you! Then you had to jump out for a rope
and slide down it to the ground. It almost shook me
up, but I went over the entire course twice. The
Slide-for-Life (where you get wet if you fall) was
fun! It was forty-five feet up at the top with four feet
of water beneath you. Some guys fell on their own,
but the DIs had fun making other guys fall by calling them to attention while they were on the ropes.
It was hilarious! Of course I guess it wouldn't have
been so funny to me if I had been one of those they
picked on, but luckily I escaped! There are some pictures of the course in the base paper I sent home, if
it's still there.

Something must be happening in Vietnam
because a lot of people here are getting shipped
over. Our Senior Drill Instructor is leaving in about
two weeks and they've guaranteed some of us would
be there with him within the next two or three
months.

This evening we packed for the rifle range and tomorrow morning we'll march out there. We will continue to get mail out there as usual, so please keep writing.

I've gotta go for now. Everybody take care and write if you can.

Love, Mike

6

This is my rifle. There are many like it but this one is mine. My rifle is my best friend. It is my life. I must master it as I master my life.

My rifle, without me is useless. Without my rifle, I am useless. I must fire my rifle true. I must shoot straighter than my enemy who is trying to kill me. I must shoot him before he shoots me. I will.

My rifle and myself know that what counts in this war is not the rounds we fire, the noise of our burst, nor the smoke we make. We know that it is the hits that count. We will hit.

My rifle is human, even as I, because it is my life. Thus, I will learn it as a brother. I will learn its weakness, its strength, its parts, its accessories, its sights, and its barrel. I will keep my rifle clean and ready, even as I am clean and ready. We will become part of each other. We will.

Before God I swear this creed. My rifle and myself are the defenders of my country. We are the

masters of our enemy. We are the saviors of my life.
So be it, until victory is America's and there is no
enemy, but Peace!
— "RIFLEMAN'S CREED" BY MAJOR GENERAL W. H. RUPERT,
UNITED STATES MARINE CORPS

We have learned that every Marine, from the lowliest private newly graduated from boot camp, to the Commandant of the Marine Corps, is first and foremost a rifleman. No matter what one's military occupational specialty (MOS) might be—cook, clerk, driver, mechanic, etc.—*all* marines are ready and able at all times to take up arms and fight effectively. This ability is a common thread running throughout the Corps.

The rifleman is the backbone of the Marine Corps. We have been at the rifle range for nearly two weeks now and have become riflemen at the expense of our *own* backbones! We have been pushed, pressed, bent, twisted, wrenched, sat on, threatened, and cajoled into positions of firing that would cause a carnival contortionist to reconsider his calling. The first week's "snapping in" period is well named. Although it is Marine Corps lingo for practice, "snapping in" could well refer to our tendons, ligaments, and bones. They have been snapped into places heretofore thought impossible, by the Marines' Chiropractic Corps—the rifle range instructors.

Having survived our week of skeletal manipulation and rearrangement, we have been live-firing for the past five days. I had really been looking forward to this part of our training, having enjoyed hunting all my life and being fairly proficient with my twenty-two-caliber rifle and single-shot shotgun. With such past expertise I figured I would have little trouble mastering the M-14.

On Monday I fired a two hundred (out of a possible two hundred fifty), which is a qualifying "marksman" score. That was a good score considering that the "dope" (elevation and windage) of my rifle hadn't been fine-tuned yet. I shot several good, tight patterns that drew a rare compliment from one of the range instructors. The next day it stormed and my score dropped to one ninety-two, still a qualifying score and not bad for the conditions and my limited experience with the M-14. Less than half of our platoon shot qualifying scores during Tuesday's high winds and rain.

Wednesday dawned clear and calm and I responded with an "expert" score of two hundred twenty. And then Thursday I topped that with a two twenty-six, which was the highest score in the platoon for the day. I was flying high—I couldn't miss. My confidence soared above Mt. Everest. Visions of shooting two hundred thirty and two hundred forty danced through my head in last night's dreams. I saw the regimental commander pinning my expert's badge to my pride-swollen chest and presenting me with a citation declaring PFC Helms the top rifleman on the entire Island! I could hardly sleep waiting for the morrow when my best friend and I would show the rest what it was all about.

Well, today was qualification day. The day when the scores would count. The day to turn hopes and dreams into reality. We would live or die for a year with our performance today on the firing line. And I *choked*. I struck out with the bases loaded to end the game. Make room, Mudville, for I have become a disgraced teammate of the infamous mighty Casey. I don't even know what happened. I was shooting great through over half of the course when suddenly it seemed I couldn't hit a bull's-eye to save my young ass. I don't know if I accidentally knocked the windage or elevation knobs and messed up my rifle's dope or what. I can't blame the weather. It was a perfectly clear day, a little windy maybe, but nothing to really mess up my shooting. Some other guys in the platoon who had been shooting well all week dropped down also. And a couple of guys who had been having "Maggie's drawers" waved at them regularly surprised everybody and fired qualifying scores.

Oh well, all is not lost. At least I shot a two hundred and seven, which qualifies me as a marksman. But damn! I know I should have shot expert, or at least sharpshooter. Shit! I dropped nineteen points. I am really pissed at myself. There's no use crying over spilt milk, but I'm afraid my chances of making PFC just flew out of the window with my expert's badge.

We have a new Senior Drill Instructor. His name is Gunnery Sergeant Weber. He is of average height and has a slight, wiry build. His face is leathery and stern and sometimes his dark eyes have a faraway, haunted look. He has just recently returned from a tour in Vietnam and has already gained our respect and admiration. The platoon is becoming quite "salty" now, but our new Senior DI handles us well. He can be hard as hell when he needs to, but he seems to be extremely fair. We like him.

Staff Sergeant Burns is meaner and nastier than ever. He must really be fuming because he didn't get moved up to Senior Drill Instructor. He seems intent on venting his wrath on us. But that's okay, because we have been made tough and salty by the brine of hard work, sweat, and esprit de corps, and we can take anything the worthless bastard dishes out.

We have moved off the rifle range to another part of the Island for a week of mess duty. By luck of the draw or favor of the gods we have been assigned to the women Marines' mess hall for our stint of KP. We cannot believe our luck. This is too good to be true. The BAMs! Broad-assed Marines. Real, live females. Objects of late night fantasies (the salt-peter has not been totally effective). It has been two months since any of us have delved into the delights of a delicious damsel. We envision Marilyn Monroe and Raquel Welch in olive drab, with swaying hips and sultry smiles. We are sorely disillusioned. What we get is Hilda Hippo, Martha Moose, and Jane B. Plain. There are, to be honest, a few good-lookers in the ranks. But they are like lepers to us anyway, strictly forbidden and untouchable. We will have to be content for the time being with the ever-faithful Rosa Palm to satisfy our youthful primeval passions.

Sunday, March 19, 1967

Dear Mama,

Well, only ten more days left until graduation. I'm sorry for not writing, but mess duty has kept us real busy. It's been worth it though, because we have hardly spent any time with our DIs this past week. So in a way it's been our easiest week since we got here.

Tonight we wrote out the nine men we thought

should get promoted to PFC. I voted for myself because I really believe I deserve it. I've scored high in almost everything we've done, and haven't failed anything. I think that not shooting expert has probably ruined my chances though, but at least I qualified.

This is going to be a really busy week. We've got Elliott's Beach, drown-proofing, Battalion Drill Competition, final field inspection and a whole bunch more stuff to do besides graduate in the next ten days. So, I'll probably not have another chance to write, but I'll try.

Y'all are not supposed to write for about the last four or five days because it'll mess up the postal system.

Are y'all still coming to graduation? If so, who all is coming? Hope to see y'all then.

Love, Mike

Gunnery Sergeant Weber has called for a platoon counsel this evening. He sits on a footlocker in the center of the squad bay and we are seated around him on the wooden deck like braves encircling their chief. A sullen mood hangs over the platoon like storm clouds which have spoiled a long-planned and much-awaited outing. We have lost the Battalion Drill Competition. It was not a mediocre performance which cost us the contest. To the contrary, our platoon executed the marching maneuvers and manual-of-arms with almost flawless skill and precision. Victory slipped from our grasp when Gunnery Sergeant Weber failed to give us a command for a manual-of-arms movement which resulted in our routine being incomplete. We had rehearsed the competition routine for endless hours, and everyone realized immediately that our Senior DI had screwed up. He knew it too, of course, but there was nothing we could do but instantly obey the out-of-sequence command he had given us. It has left a bitter taste in our mouths to know we are the best but won't receive the recognition because of a technical screw-up. Gunnery Sergeant Weber breaks the silence.

"Privates, what happened out there today was my fault. I take full responsibility and blame for losing the competition. I met with the judges this afternoon and they told me that we would have won this thing if I hadn't failed to give the command to order arms. I have no excuse, privates. I just fucked up. But they also said that I have one highly motivated and squared-away herd. When you men obeyed the command I gave without hesitation, even though you all knew it was wrong, it impressed the hell out of the judges. Privates, that's what it's all about—instant obedience without question. That's what can mean the difference between living or dying in combat. I couldn't be more proud of you than if that trophy was sitting right here in our laps now. You men are winners!"

Private Hatcher, our platoon right-guide, jumps up and calls the platoon to attention. We scramble to our feet and snap-to.

"Sir, Private Hatcher requests permission to speak to the Senior Drill Instructor, Sir!"

"Speak, Private Hatcher."

"Sir, the privates of Platoon Two Forty-two are proud to have the Senior Drill Instructor as their leader, Sir!"

The platoon erupts into cheers and war whoops that threaten to shatter the windows and crumble the plaster of the aged barracks. A genuine smile breaks the usual grim sternness of Gunnery Sergeant Weber's weathered face.

"Thank you, privates. I'm proud of each and every one of you. You're going to make damn good marines. Now, turn-to and get this area squared away and ready for lights out, or I'm going to start kicking some asses!"

The smile has disappeared, but a betraying twinkle remains in the normally vacant eyes. We turn-to.

Final inspection is tomorrow, and we are standing tall before our racks while our DIs go over us with the proverbial fine-toothed comb in a dress rehearsal. Oh, Christ! Burns has my section. He holds a bright bare lightbulb attached to a long extension cord and is checking us for close shaves. Hey, no sweat. All I've got is a little peach fuzz anyway. I sure pity the guys with heavy beards. He stops in front of me. My stomach muscles tighten reflexively as he taps my chin upward with the back of his hand.

"You missed a spot right there, maggot!"

I cry out in surprised pain and instinctively back away, clutching the area of my neck he has just burned with his white-hot branding iron. He grabs me by the collar and roughly jerks me forward.

"Don't pull away from me, shitbird! And here's another spot you missed!"

I grit my teeth in a painful wince as another section of my neck is branded. I will not give the sorry son of a bitch the pleasure of hearing me cry out again.

"Now get your worthless ass to the head and shave that shit off!"

I stare into the mirror at my inflamed neck, searching for the cause of my misfortune. I find nothing but clean-shaven skin, now decorated with two reddened and welted circles.

Graduation day! The impossible, unattainable dream of long ago has finally materialized. The disorganized, motley crowd of disheveled youths that stumbled off those buses in disbelieving shock ten weeks before no longer exists. We have been miraculously transformed into a tightly organized and disciplined unit reflecting the finest in military bearing and character.

We stand proud and tall in our smart dress-green uniforms as Major General Tompkins, the Commanding General of Parris Island Marine Recruit Training Depot, sings our praises and reminds us of the high standards and traditions of the Corps which we are now responsible to uphold at all costs.

The Marine Corps builds men. The Green Machine has done its work well. We have earned the title. From this day forward, we are full-fledged *United States Marines*.

The command is given: "Drill Instructors, dismiss your platoons."

"Platoon Two Forty-two," bellows Gunnery Sergeant Weber, *"dismissed!"*

Cheers and piss-cutters fill the air, and we head into an uncertain future.

7

The humming drone of the jet engines has lulled me into an advanced stage of drowsiness. I shift into a more upright position in my window seat and force myself awake with an exaggerated stretch and wide-mouthed yawn. I don't want to sleep through this trip. First time across the great big U.S. of A. I've never been out of the South before. Big adventure time. I don't want to miss a thing. See and do it all. Grab for all the gusto while I can. I damn well better, because the chances are good that I'll never live to see twenty.

Headed across the Big Pond for an all-expenses-paid thirteen-month vacation in that tropical paradise called Vietnam. But first there's two weeks in golden California. Hollywood, movie stars, Disneyland, bikini-clad beach bunnies, Tijuana! Of course, the Crotch will insist on throwing in a little jungle warfare training here and there, but I can't let that minor inconvenience spoil my fun. Eat, drink and be merry, for tomorrow we die. There it is!

I look out the window. Big, beautiful country down

there. Too bad I can't see it. Nothing but billowy white clouds below. Like floating over an endless cotton field. Boll weevil heaven.

Long, sleek, angled silver wing catches my eye. Beautiful damn airliner. Engine is still attached. Far cry from the rickety old prop jobs I've flown up and down the East Coast. I swear I've seen the rivets on the wings vibrate and fall off! On one flight the damn turbine engine belched smoke and flame the whole time. Nothing to worry about, the stewardess said. Scared me shitless. White-knuckle city. It's a wonder the whole fuselage didn't come apart in that turbulence. This is much better. This airline has got its head and ass wired together. I can almost relax.

Young stewardess catches my eye. Damn, she's good-looking. Walking over to me.

"Is there anything I can get you, Marine?" The soft words roll off a velvety tongue and through smiling lips that beg to be kissed.

Fucking-A! Come sit on my lap and let's talk about the first thing that pops up. . . . "No thank you, ma'am, I'm fine."

Like hell I'm fine—I'm hornier than a goddamn desert toad. Have mercy on a poor young patriotic Marine, ma'am, who will soon probably die for his country so that you can continue to fly across this great land of freedom. Take me back to your lounge and relieve my misery. Don't let me die without a final tasting of young American womanhood. Let me slip into eternity with the memory of our passionate high-altitude escapade fresh on my mind, and a shit-eating grin on my face. Then, I will not have died in vain. I will have given my all for my country; you can give *your* all to me. How about it, honey? That's the least you could do for the war effort.

Bentley stirs in the seat beside me, his soft snoring changing momentarily to a strangled gurgle. He coughs and swallows hard, clearing his throat. The snoring resumes. He's been sleeping damn near the whole flight. He boarded the plane in New Orleans, drunk as a skunk. Been partying the whole night, he said. He probably had a whole six-pack. Can't hold his booze worth a shit. Advantages to being a cheap drunk though, especially when you only make around a hundred dollars a month.

We've been together our entire ten-month military careers. Good feeling of security to have someone you know and trust to go through this shit with. The Marine Corps, in a brilliant display of military wisdom, made us both office pogues after boot camp. A real damn kick in the ass! Both of us joined the Crotch to fight, so they make us a couple of desk jockeys. I would've joined the Air Force if I'd had aspirations to be a pencil-pusher.

After infantry training at Camp Geiger, me and Bentley got stationed at Camp Lejeune, North Carolina, pounding typewriters. A couple of regular Remington Raiders! Never-ending boredom and bullshit. Immediately started filling out requests for transfer to the infantry. Took all summer, but they finally came through. Change of MOS to the grunts, and orders for FMF WESPAC. Another jaunt through ITR for more advanced infantry training, twenty days' leave, and we're on our way.

Bentley's a good dude and a good Marine. Made PFC out of boot camp, and just recently made lance corporal. I made PFC shortly after arriving at Lejeune to push paper.

Looks like he'll probably stay one step ahead of me, promotion-wise. He's a year older than me, and always seems to have his shit together. From Mobile, Alabama. Looks a little bull-doggish, like Gunny Franz. He'll make a great-looking DI some day, if he lives long enough and decides to re-up.

Doesn't intimidate me, though. I know him too well. Had to nurse him through a bad drunk a couple of months ago after he got that letter from his longtime girlfriend:

"Dear John, I'll always love you but you're going overseas to get your ass shot off and besides I can't possibly wait thirteen months so I've decided to go ahead and end our relationship which I'll always cherish and by-the-way I'm fucking your best friend Jody. Love ya, Susie Rottencrotch."

Damn bitch almost ruined the boy. He'll make it, though. One hard hombre.

I keep having second thoughts about my valorous jump to the grunts. Probably could have skated my entire enlistment in that office at Lejeune. And now, because of my own insistence and stupidity, I have become one of Them—*the Few, the Proud, the Condemned—the Grunts!* Most grunts would give their left nut to have the job I had. Way to go, Mikey. Another magnificent fuck-up. Keep it up boy, you'll get your young ass waxed yet.

Bentley's stirring, waking up now. He yawns deeply, a foul wind smacks me square in the face. Jesus, smells like a goat shit in his mouth. Blood-shot eyes gaining focus, foggy mind trying to recognize surroundings. Punches me in the shoulder and grins.

"Hey stud, how's it going? Where the hell we at now?"

I look out the window. No break in the deep cloud blanket yet. "We're just passing over Bugfuck, New Mexico." Serious answer, fighting off the urge to break out laughing.

Bentley nods his head in affirmation, smacking dry lips and cottony tongue in a vain effort to expel goat shit and find a trace of moisture. He still must be half-asleep to have bought that bullshit. Usually much too sharp to fall for such a line of crap.

"Man, I'm dying of thirst. Where's that fucking broad at?" All females of the species have become "fucking broads" to Bentley since his "Dear John" letter. He catches stewardess of my fantasy's attention and tells her to bring him a beer. The lady definitely has her house in order. Sweetly, she informs him that they'll soon be serving lunch and talks him into having a Coke instead. I settle for a Coke too, although from staring at the fullness beneath her white blouse I was tempted to ask for a shot of milk served from the natural container. Probably would have slapped me silly. I've gotta watch this fantasizing shit—it's doing nothing but giving me a bad case of the blue-balls. Young man's malady. Only one cure. Come heal me, honey. Shit, there I go again.

Finished our lunch of club sandwiches, potato chips and dill pickle slices. Pretty damn good, but I could have easily eaten three helpings. Still have a voracious appetite. Gained fourteen pounds in boot camp, all muscle. I weigh over one eighty-five now. Participated in athletics all my life, but I've never been in better shape. Crotch does indeed build men, at least in body. Shit, mind and spirit, too. Why would a sane man leave a plush desk job to go halfway around the world to chase gooks through steaming jungles and stinking rice paddies? Yep, they got my mind, too. And my spirit. I volunteered for this shit!

Jerry Lewis flick playing on the screen. Ain't this some shit? Movies on airplanes. Bentley's sleeping again, and I'm having trouble concentrating on the movie. I usually love Jerry Lewis comedies, but other things have wrested control of my mind. What will it really be like? Training films didn't seem too bad, even saw some wounded guys. They didn't seem too scared. Seen plenty of John Wayne flicks in my time. Wonder how close they are to the real thing? What's it really like to be shot at? Had live rounds fired overhead in training. Wasn't too bad. Planted charges blew up all around us to simulate incoming mortars and artillery. Noisy as hell and showered us with dirt, but no hot shrapnel whizzing through the air. I wonder how close that was to the real shit? Must be pretty realistic. Why else would they use those methods to train us? After all, the Marines are supposed to have the best training in the world. Feel better about it now. Came through all those training exercises with flying colors. Probably do okay in the real shit, too. Maybe. I hope so.

Wish Rip Van Winkle would wake up and talk to me. Nothing seems to bother that asshole. Sleep through anything. I need to talk. Thinking much too much. Left home just this morning and I'm already lonely and getting depressed. Mother, brothers and sister saw me off. Brave fronts all around. Wonder if I'll ever see them again? I might damn well not. Thirteen months is a long time to cheat fate. Most grunts make it, though. I probably will. Maybe not.

I see the headlines: *Local Grunt Gets His Shit Blown*

Away in Republic of Vietnam. Body bag city. Next stop—
Evergreen Cemetery. Planted six feet under near the old
man. Wonderful future. Died for his country, they'll say.
Yeah, deader than shit. Play taps, hand over the flag and
forget him. Should have gone to college anyway. Had a
chance at a baseball scholarship. Joined the Crotch
instead. His choice. Now he's got to live with it. Except
he's deader than a doornail—forever! Maybe he's resting
now in the sweet arms of Jesus. Probably just maggot-bait.
Ashes to ashes, dust to dust, shit to shit. Amen.

No Smoking sign flashes on. Object of infatuation
reminds everyone to fasten their seat belt. Death-grip on
armrests during noticeably steep descent. Slow this thing
down!

Los Angeles area visible now. Dirty haze hangs over
much of the city. My first glimpse of smog. This place is
huge! Exciting. Objects on the ground quickly getting bigger and bigger. Scary. Hope that son of a bitch of a pilot
knows what he's doing. Looks like we're gonna land in the
middle of a bunch of skyscrapers. Shit! Headlines change:
Local Grunt Dies in Los Angeles Plane Crash.

Area clearing. Open spaces. Plane leveling off, floating
above immense runway. Gentle touchdown. Taxiing
toward terminal. Seat belts off. Farewell, beautiful lady, it
would have been so nice.

Step out into bright sunshine. California, here I
come.

8

Inside the airport terminal now. This place is like a city unto itself. It is enormous. Never seen anything like it. I thought Atlanta was big, but this is astounding. Must be more people in here than there are back home in all of Bay County. Can't believe it. All kinds, too. Looks like a damn United Nations convention or something. A regular Heinz 57 Varieties.

We leave our sea bags in check, cram our AWOL bags inside a rental locker and jump aboard one of the many trams traversing the vast hallways carrying passengers to and from the far reaches of this colossal travelers' domain.

"Well stud, whatcha say we grab us a couple of beers and unwind a little. Damn plane ride wore my young ass out." Bentley seems to be his old self again, taking charge.

"Fucking-A. Best idea you've had all day." *Only* idea you've had all day, you sleep-saturated son of a bitch.

Two old ladies in the car ahead of us glance back, frowning. Look perturbed. Gotta watch this Marine Corps' jargon around civilians. Crotch has turned us into foul-mouthed motherfuckers.

Lounge sighted up ahead. Time to disembark. Off the tram and into the pleasant darkness. We find a corner booth and slide in. Clanging of glasses, low rumbling conversations and high-pitched falsetto of Motown soul fills the smoky air. Smokey Robinson and the Miracles, I think. Not my style, but fits the atmosphere of the place.

Eyes adjusting to the dimness. The room is a crowded hodgepodge. Marines and sailors well represented. Lots of civilians of various races and dress. A few Army and Air Force personnel thrown in for good measure. Hope they don't check our IDs. Screwed if they do.

Waitress coming over. Nice legs showing below the black velvet mini-skirt. Eyes wandering upward. Slim hips, trim waist. Nothing to complain about yet. Further up. Meaty cleavage from obvious push-up bra bulging above low-cut white silk blouse. This shit's getting serious. Fantasy Land starting up again. On up. Round face with heavily made-up eyes and lips, framed by teased bouffant hairdo. Fantasy over. Looks like Petunia Pig. An *old* pig. Must be in her thirties.

Bentley seems enthralled. Laying a heavy dose of southern gentleman bullshit on her. Wants her damn life history, for christ sakes. All I want is a beer. Come on, asshole, must be ten million broads in southern California that look better than this porker. We've only got three days before we have to report to Camp Pendleton, and you're trying to bang a boar. Headline: *Bulldog Boom-Booms Bacon!* What is this shit—no screw, no brew? Oh, I get it. He isn't so dumb after all. He's sweet-

talking us right out of an ID check. Got his shit together, as usual. Must be why he's a lance corporal and
I'm just a lowly PFC. Outstanding, Bentley. Two Coors
on the way.

Cab ride from the airport was interesting. Driver was a
good dude. Pointed out some sights for us along the way,
and told us where to go to find the action. World War Two
veteran. Talked a lot about the "Big One." Served with the
Army in the Pacific Theater. Helped liberate the Philippines. Said he really felt for us, where we're going. Country doesn't seem to be behind the effort. Not like WWII,
when everybody joined the effort and made sacrifices.
Nobody seems to really care about this one. Sort of like
Korea, but worse. Glad he only has daughters. Doesn't
know what he'd do if he had a son that had to go. Said he
really respected us for being Marines and volunteering
and all that patriotic shit. A whole world apart from the
drug-crazy hippies that fill the streets and colleges around
here. Said we helped restore his belief in America's youth.
Left us feeling in limbo, somewhere between patriotism
and desertion.

All checked-in at the Caravan Motel, Anaheim, California. Beautiful room on the second deck. Two big double
beds. Fancy carpet. Nicely furnished, even has a color television. Never had one when I was a kid. Always wanted
one, but had to be content with black and white. This
thing's got a channel on every click of the knob. I used to
only get one channel back home. Tempted to lay here and
just watch TV for three days.

* * *

It's late in the evening. We are lounging around the pool area feeling somewhere between mellow and shit-faced. Watching with laid-back interest a few motel guests still using the pool in the slight chill of the October night. Newlywed couple keeps hugging and kissing and rubbing all over each other. Hey dude, you wanna trade places? You go to Vietnam and fight Charlie, and I'll stay here and douse your spouse with all kinds of love and affection. How 'bout it, asshole? Nah, he'd never go for it. Screw him *and* her. What-the-fuck do they know anyway? They don't know *shit*. Rich daddy probably paid for their honeymoon. They'll probably go back home in a week or two and start protesting the war on some liberal college campus in Jerk Off, U.S. of A. Assholes.

Bentley and Bendix are passed out. Pitiful looking ass-holes hanging half on and half off the lounge chairs. Duvall is singing some goddamn cowboy song in the most obnoxious voice I've ever heard. Something about a lonely cowboy out on the prairie, screwing a cow 'cause his girl-friend got married, or some such shit. Bentley should hear this. Son of a bitch could put the cocksucking coyotes out of business, big-time. As foul a howl as you'd never want to hear. Shit!

I grope for another beer in the Styrofoam ice chest. Coors. Good shit. Can't get it back home. Pop-a-top-again time. Through the lips and over the tongue, look out stomach, here it comes. Empty cans litter our area, but ain't nobody fucked with us yet. If they do we'll wax their asses. Fucking-A! Getting drunker than a skunk and don't give a royal rat's ass. Shit. Let them go fight the fucking war and we'll run their goddamn plush motel for 'em.

Call it the Marines' Motel, or the Grunts' Grovel. There it is!

Duvall has finished his sadistic serenade. His eyes are struggling to stay open. Pours a beer more down his chest than his throat. Good dudes, Bendix and Duvall. Went through ITR retraining together. Set up rendezvous with them here. They actually showed up—out-fucking-standing! Good thing, too. Duvall's twenty-one and can supply all the booze we want, and we definitely want all the booze he can supply. Gotta get it while the getting's good. We're all gonna be dead shortly. Got just a few days to make up for fifty years of partying. They're both from Wisconsin. Not bad dudes, for Yankees. Grew up sucking cow titties, I guess. Dairyland, U.S. of A.

Oh, shit! Duvall's throwing-up all over the area. Puke puddles forming beneath his lounging rack. Streaming down his throat, across his chest and forming weird patterns that change with every heave.

Enough of this shit. Into the chlorine pond I go. Cold water helps shake the cobwebs from my head. That's better. Now, if I can just make it out of the pool and back to the lounger.

I stumble off the trail again, bend over and puke my guts out for the umpteenth time. Foul, slimy bile-green liquid rushes up my throat and spews violently out of my mouth onto the burnished grass of the California hilltop. My heavy field transport pack threatens to push my shoulders and face into the disgusting deluge. Oh, god! Please just let me die. Another one of those "Please, Lord, if you'll only let me live through this one I swear I'll never do it again" ecclesiastical bullshit situations. Classical "dance to the music, pay the piper" predicament. Oh, god, did I ever dance! And christ, am I ever paying! Never again. I swear. I *really* mean it this time, God. I wouldn't bullshit you, Lord! Won't somebody please just shoot me and put me out of my misery?

The word comes down the column to fall out and take ten. Somebody up there must have been listening. I crawl under a low bush to escape the blistering sun and roll over on my back, using the burden I've been humping all morning for support. Ahh, that's better. Nausea temporarily fading away. Cool shade and gentle breeze. Feels good against my sweat-soaked utilities. Wonder how Bentley and the others are hacking this shit. Must be suffering too. God, what a night! Mind wondering back over the past few days. . . .

The day after the pool side fiasco we sobered up enough to make it to Disneyland by late morning. Had a great time. Last-gasp effort at being kids before we die or have our youth snatched from us. Really got into the spirit of the place. Even enjoyed the kiddie rides, especially the flying Dumbo the Elephant. Rode that one three times.

Sat near some high school girls on the Jungle Cruise. Flirted with them. Big macho Marine bullshit—going to fight for their freedom, probably won't make it back, etc. Fell for it, but learned their parents were around somewhere. Didn't need that scene. Funny, they were only a year or two younger than me, but they seemed so silly and I felt so much older. Strange.

Planned to stay until closing, but had to leave about an hour before. Duvall had snuck in a couple of pints and got smashed. Tried to put the make on Snow White during the evening parade down Main Street, U.S.A. She was friendly, but security guards weren't. Strongly advised to escort one drunken Marine off premises. Advice heeded. Good time, anyway.

Slept late and laid around the motel area all day Sunday. Reported to Pendleton Monday. Reunion with all the guys from our ITR company. Looks like we're all going over together. Busy week of jungle warfare classes, squad tactics, fire and maneuver and weapons familiarity. Idiotic Marine Corps spends endless hours teaching us the M-14 rifle inside and out, and now they tell us we're going to be using this plastic piece of shit M-16 in Vietnam. Fucking incredible. Par-for-the-militaristic-bullshit-course.

Liberty for the weekend. We four musketeers rode a bus to Oceanside and rented a room near the beach. Spent most of Saturday by the long concrete pier watching hot-dog surfers do their thing and deeply tanned beach bunnies swing and jiggle theirs. Nice, but no score. Not impressed one bit by "Marines heading overseas" stories. Seemed very turned off, in fact. Short hair and war evidently not their bag. Oh well.

Rented a car the next day and headed for Tijuana. Stopped in a combination lounge and package store in San Diego. Had a few drafts and got a couple of six-packs to go. Poked fun at the swabbies. Asked them where we could get us one of those cute little clown suits they wear. Good-natured retorts. Marines and sailors love to hate each other. Diego crawling with them.

On to T-town. Left car on our side of the border and crossed over on foot. Too big a risk to drive over. Long walk through hovel-crowded hills to town. Downtown area a big contrast to the impoverished outskirts. Neon lights flashing gaudy colors against the purplish Mexican twilight. Streets, shops and bars bustling with activity. Hawkers in garish suits beckoning passersby to come in and see "the best show in town." Leering glances through open doorways at numerous dancers in varying stages of undress. Not too bad. Accosted by hordes of ten-year-old pimps trying to peddle their "sisters" for a few American dollars. Amazing shit. Sure as hell looked like the action wouldn't be hard to find. It wasn't.

First stop a dive called the Thunderbird Club. Immediately hustled into a booth in a dark corner by four giggling barmaids. Jesus, their hands were *everywhere!* Glad we listened to sage advice of others and kept most of our money stuffed in our socks. Rock and roll band blasting on the jukebox. Drinks for all. Soon apparent that these broads weren't groping for our money, at least directly. Can't believe this shit—right here in the damn booth!

Sultry whispered offers of much more action upstairs penetrate our ears along with tickling tongues. Duvall the first to go, holding his jacket over his crotch and grinning like a buzzard on a body wagon. Bendix trying to talk prices with his passion princess. Cheap son of a bitch. What the hell is five dollars anyway? Bentley's ranting and raving about "fucking broads" again. Scared the shit out of his senorita. Adios, crazy amigo.

Adjusted eyes give me a better look at my young Mexican maiden. Ugh! Looks like Milton Berle in drag. No thank you, ma'am. I'll just have another beer, please. . . .

Great place, that Hawaiian A'Go-Go! Sharp-looking

Mexican cuties in cages bumping and grinding to the sounds of a live rock-and-roll band. Sang some in Spanish, some in English. Fairly well on my way to a good drunk by this time. Those Zombies were good. Never had one before. All kinds of booze poured by layers into a tall, frosty glass. Good shit. One after another. Danced and cohorted for hours. Good-looking stuff in this place. A trip or two to the rooms out back. Great duty, man. No need for ol' Rosa Palm if you get stationed out here! Bendix had a good-looking young broad with him. I walked over, planted a big kiss and stole her away. Just like that. Take what you want and fuck the rest. There it is! Got himself another one right away, though. Pickings real good in there.

All four drunker than hell, staggering around trying to find famous donkey and woman act. Don't believe we found it. Don't remember it if we did. Saw one great show, though. Remember that one well. Simply amazing. Broad performed all kinds of tricks with that thing. It smoked a cigarette, made a quart milk bottle disappear, and picked up a silver dollar that was laying flat on a stool. Out-fucking-standing! Best damn event of the night. Cheered and cheered.

Rest of the night very foggy. So drunk. Another trip to a palace of passion, more bars, more strip shows. Almost got in a fight when Duvall bit a dancer right on the muff while she was grinding it in his face. Lots of Marines and swabbies in the place. Only thing that saved our young asses. Might still be in the T-town slammer otherwise.

Lying in the backseat, puking all the way back to Oceanside. Floorboard sloshing with vomit last clear thought I have. No recollection of how we got on the bus and back to our barracks. 0330 when we hit the rack. Reveille was at 0500. Really great way to prepare for a ten-mile hump up and down these hills with full combat gear and packs. Way to go, Mikey, you did it again!

Oh, those goddamn Zombies. I'll never even *look* at one of those things again. Great name for them, though. I *feel* like a fucking zombie. No I don't. Zombies are dead, and death couldn't *possibly* feel as bad as this. Shit, I wish I *was* dead.

Word is passed to saddle up. Time to resume our pleasant little stroll through the hills. I struggle to my feet and wrestle the pack straps into a less-tortuous position. Hot glaring sun again. Nausea returning. Oh, shit—dry heaves this time. Nothing left to puke up.

I see Bentley up the trail, bent over and heaving. I break into a wide grin. Not suffering alone. Misery loves company.

9

"Hey, man . . . youse scared?" The whispered, almost timid question comes out of the blackness from the rear of the dank bunker.

Good question. I haven't really thought about it yet. Been too busy and fascinated with this whole scene to think about particulars. I better come up with some kind of an answer, though. This kid seems real jumpy. And it's my ass that'll be on the line when he takes his turn on watch. Don't want him getting *my* shit blown away before I've had time to figure out what the hell's going on here myself. Guess I'll lie a little bit.

"No, man. No reason to be scared here. This ain't the bush. Just keep your head down and your eyes and ears open. Charlie ain't likely to fuck with us here."

Damn, what an answer. Sounded real confident and assuring. Almost believe my own bullshit. Probably close to being correct, though. The NVA and VC would have to be crazy to try a ground assault on this place. There's been some incoming from across the DMZ each day since I got here, and a few harassing mortar rounds at night. Nothing serious. But a ground assault? No way. They'd get greased before they ever got within a hundred meters of the wire. The firepower we've got here is unbelievable.

Another flare from the 81mm mortars section pops several hundred meters beyond the perimeter, bathing the darkness with its eerie orange glow as it sizzles and sways beneath the silk parachute. Somewhere in the distance to the northwest sporadic gunfire and the occasional boom of explosions interrupt the otherwise excessive quietness of the area.

I've been here at Dong Ha just below the DMZ for four days now, in-country for five. Work details during the day and perimeter duty at night while I wait for my outfit to come back off an operation. Been assigned to Second Battalion, Fourth Marines. Supposed to be a good outfit. Seen plenty of action in this war. Just came down from a place called Con Thien after a couple of months of heavy fighting. Lot of casualties, I heard. I'm anxious as hell to join them. Hope I fit in okay. Those guys have seen a lot of shit and I'll be the FNG—fucking new guy—on the block. What the hell. They were *all* new guys once. A couple of months and a few firefights under my belt and I'll be an old salt teaching replacements the ropes myself.

"Where youse from?" Lampley, the nervous guy, is trying to make conversation again. He just got here this afternoon. Flew into Danang this morning, got processed and caught a quick flight up North, and here he is. He's still wearing stateside utilities and boots. Fresh out of boot camp and ITR. Just turned eighteen last month, he said. Looks about twelve.

"Florida. How about you?" It's still early, and my watch, so I'll humor him. Besides, I know the lonely feeling of the first night.

"Pennsylvania, just outside Philly."

I knew it. That accent. Just like Corporal Mathis from the office me and Bentley were stuck in at Camp Lejeune.

Bentley . . . damn, I'm gonna miss being with him. First time we've been separated since our bus arrived at Parris Island. Shit, I feel like a goddamn orphan or something. I drew Two-Four and he got Two-Twenty-six. Bendix and Duvall are gone, too. I don't remember their outfits. Several guys from our old ITR unit got assigned to Two-Four with me, but none that I'm really close to.

I'm sure gonna miss that bastard Bentley. In a way I'm glad, though. It would be real tough if we were together and he got zapped and I had to see him die. He probably feels the same way. I'm *glad* the fucker's gone. Won't know shit until this whole game's over with. Sure as hell hope he makes it.

A muffled *pop!* and the latest flare casts weird shadows that dance like ghosts among the layers of concertina wire strung in front of our position. Jesus! The hair on the back of my neck raises up as a cold shudder races down my spine. Looks like somebody's in the wire! Can't be. The cans would be rattling and the pop flares would be going off if anybody was trying to get through the wire, wouldn't they?

I turn my head away from the confusing landscape and shut my eyes for a second. I blink and look back. The infiltrating specters have vanished as the flare floats farther down the line. *Shit!* Easy as hell to get spooked here! I've got a lot to learn and get used to. That's about the tenth time in four nights that's happened. Conjuring up all kinds of strange shit. Gotta get a handle on this crap.

I check the row of hand grenades lined neatly on the sandbag shelf before me. Gotta be ready. Next time it might not be my imagination crawling through the wire.

Lampley's finally calmed down enough to get some sleep. Hope he didn't notice how scared I was awhile ago. He thinks I'm an old hand at this shit. I haven't told him that I've been here less than a week. Must be the jungle boots and utilities I bought off that grunt in Okinawa the day before our flight to Danang. Slightly used and salty. Better than new. Makes me look like I've seen a little shit.

Low, crackling static sounds from the radio in our bunker as the CP calls for a situation report. I grab the handset and key it twice to indicate that everything is secure at our position.

I strain my eyes at the luminous dial of the watch I borrowed from the sergeant in charge of the bunkers in this sector. 0300. Halfway through my second two-hour watch. This gets boring after a while. Beats the hell out of the work details I've been on, though. Burning shitters. About as low as you can go on the duty roster. I've spent the last three mornings carrying halved fifty-five gallon drums sloshing full of shit and piss, pouring diesel fuel in 'em, setting 'em on fire and watching the putrid mess burn. God, what a smell! Damn wind seems to keep changing and blows the foul fumes all over me no matter how much I try to avoid it. Permeates everything it touches. Glorious goddamn job. *"What did you do in the war, Daddy?" Chest swells with pride. "I burned shit, son."* Jesus.

"Wake up, wake up, wake up!"

"Wh . . . what the fuck? What is it?" Lampley's got hold of my shoulder, shaking me awake. The whites of his eyes look big as saucers in the pitch blackness of the bunker.

"I think I see something! I'm *sure* I did!" Fast, excited voice, much too loud if there *is* something out there.

Aw, shit. He sees a shadow and ruins the best Zs I've cut since I've been here. "Where at, Lampley?" My question betrays a tinge of disgust in my voice over my interrupted sleep.

"There, over there!" Damn, he's almost shouting now. My eyes follow his pointing finger beyond the wire about midway between us and the bunker to our left.

Son of a bitch. Two small, darting figures about fifty meters beyond the concertina heading away from us! I grope in the darkness for the radio to report the movement and start to tell Lampley not to fire his rifle yet because the muzzle flash will give away our position but it's too late because the little shit is popping away with his M-16 and the gun team on our left two bunkers down is cutting loose and red tracers are streaking towards the place where the two gooks were and *Jesus H. Christ* a tremendous explosion just to our left-front the goddamn gooks must be blowing the wire shit the whole damn line is opening up now firing from every bunker more explosions to our left must be trying to knock out the gun team flares are popping everywhere night has become brilliant day and I'm firing at shadows or gooks or something outside the wire to our left where the big explosion was doesn't matter now they know where the bunkers are fucking RPGs probably gonna come crashing in and blow our shit away mortars are walking all over the area to our front outside the wire jam another magazine in my '16 cease fire cease fire somebody is yelling cease fire. . . .

We stare out at the surrealistic scene. No incoming rounds now. Flares still popping all over keeping the whole base ablaze with amber glare. Weapons back on safety. Hearts still pumping wildly, strange high on massive adrenaline rush. Sergeant and assistant going from bunker to bunker, checking for casualties and assessing the situation.

"Everything okay here?"

"Yeah," I answer. "Anybody get hit?"

"Towns and his A-gunner caught some shrapnel from a rocket. They're okay. Keep your fucking eyes open and your heads down. Hundred percent alert until daylight." They head off in a low crouch for the next bunker.

Flares coming with less frequency now. Everything quiet again along the line. Almost back to normal. My temples have quit throbbing and my heart no longer threatens to explode within my chest. Man, that was *something*. Scary . . . exciting.

Lampley stares across the bunker at me, an incredulous look on his face. "I thought youse said we wouldn't get no ground attack here!"

I stare back hard at him, then break into a big grin. "How the fuck would *I* know? I've only been here six days."

10

From within the hollow belly of the C-130 Hercules the straining roar of the engines plays havoc with our eardrums as the camouflage-painted cargo plane finally reaches the apex of its steep ascent and begins to level off. *Whew!* That's better. For awhile there I thought for sure this thing was gonna fall right on its ass and kill us all. Amazing the damned ugly thing can get off the ground at all, much less really fly. How the hell they could ever take off if this cargo deck was fully loaded is beyond me. Good thing this one is nearly empty. Just a few pallets of C-rations and crates of ammunition, and us six replacements for Echo Company.

Dykes is the only guy I know out of the bunch. All the others I know from our old ITR unit have been assigned to the other companies in our battalion—Foxtrot, Golf and Hotel. Dykes is eighteen, rather thin with fat lips and a thick New Jersey accent. "Joisey," he calls it. I don't care for him too much. I don't dislike him; we're just not really friends. Much closer to a few of the other guys going to the different companies.

We're headed for Ai Tu, a small vill near Quang Tri City where our company is providing security for a Seabee battalion while they construct a new airstrip and base. Word is that it's just far enough south of the DMZ to be out of artillery range. That'll be a pleasant change. Just the few rounds of that shit I experienced at Dong Ha is enough to convince me that one round is one round too many.

Crew chief wearing an olive drab flight suit and helmet walks nonchalantly to the rear of the plane where the cargo ramp stands half-ajar. I've been wondering about that. He idles over to the gap where one false step or slight jolt of turbulence could send him plummeting thousands of feet to an untimely demise. Stands there unconcernedly on the brink of eternity and fiddles with some buttons and switches mounted to the fuselage. No parachute. No safety line. A case of bona fide insanity if I ever saw one.

I squirm deeper into the webbing of my folding seat and grip the safety belt tightly with both hands, convinced now that this aircraft is faulty and the heavy ramp is going to fall completely off and take the rear part of the fuselage including me with it. Shit, if I'd wanted to fall out of an airplane I'd've joined the goddamn Army airborne. At least they would've provided a parachute! Crew chief finishes his precipitous piddling and ambles back up to the cockpit area.

The plane suddenly tilts forward and we begin a steep descent. Very steep. Shit, I knew it! We're gonna crash. We can't possibly be landing yet; we only took off five minutes ago. Crazy crew chief walking back toward us again, leaning forward against our dive. Looks totally unconcerned. I'm about to shit in my pants, and he looks like he's out for a pleasant stroll in the park!

Maybe we're not going to crash, after all. The hurtling hulk of the C-130 suddenly rights itself and seconds later a slight jolt and increased roaring of the engines signal our safe return to earth. Christ, I'm glad I didn't go into the air wing—I'd be a goddamn nervous wreck.

We emerge from the bowels of the aircraft and are greeted by the chilling dampness of the early monsoon. Dark, shredded curtains of clouds reach down to mingle with the gray fogginess which envelops the bleak landscape. The low, sparsely vegetated sand dunes and flats are a sharp contrast to the red clay muck of Dong Ha. A fine mist quickly coats faces, hands, clothing and equipment with a gentle wetness.

A couple of hundred meters to the west of the sectioned metal airstrip a paved road runs north and south. Must be Highway One. Beyond the road a railroad track parallels it into the distance. To the east of the airstrip is a pretty, winding river. Several layers of coiled concertina wire have been strung around the entire area, marking a crude perimeter. At the north end of the runway heavy equipment rumbles as Seabees work to extend its length. In every direction scattered Marines are busy filling sandbags to shore-up hastily constructed bunkers and sleeping hooches.

A jeep comes speeding across the tarmac and skids to a sliding stop a few feet away. A tall, lanky Marine hops out and grins. "Any of you guys for Echo?"

"Yeah, all of us."

"Jump in. I'm Corporal Sharpe, former grunt and now very short company clerk. Anybody here from California?"

Florida, Mississippi, New Jersey, New York and two from Missouri. No Californians. Should've known he was a Hollywood Marine from the way he drives. Must've been a damn stunt driver in civilian life.

We speed along down the runway toward a group of tents clustered in the distance. "You guys will like it here," Sharpe says, talking loudly above the jeep's engine and the humming of the knobby tires on the metal surface. "Not much happening since we got here. Mostly short patrols, ambushes and LPs. Catch a few mortars and sniper rounds, but that's about it. Get to eat in the Seabee's mess hall once in a while. The chow is number-fucking-one."

Jesus, he makes it sound like a damn picnic—"just some mortars and snipers, nothing to worry about"— christ, as if you can't get wasted by a mortar or sniper! This guy must've really seen some shit. My curiosity's got the better of me. I've got to ask: "Heard y'all were up at Con Thien a while back. How was it?"

His pleasant, almost exuberant expression suddenly goes blank. A hollow, far away look replaces it. Silence for an awful moment. Jesus, I'm sorry I asked. Turns his head toward me.

"Con Thien sucks."

I feel like a complete asshole. Way to go, Mikey. Real smart move, boy. How to win friends and influence people.

We turn off the runway and down a sandy lane between rows of big, heavy canvas tents. Sharpe pulls over and stops in front of a tent whose sides are surrounded by a wall of stacked sandbags.

"Company CP," Sharpe announces. "I'll introduce you guys to the Top. He'll get you processed and assigned to your platoons."

Glad to see his mood has swung back to where it was before my stupid question. Curious again. "How long you got left on your tour?"

Ear-to-ear shit-eating grin. "Two days and a wake-up, my man. Two days and a wake-up!"

Lucky bastard.

Crack! The sudden and unexpected blast of a rifle from somewhere across the river causes me to flinch and duck my head momentarily below the surface of the perimeter bunker where I'm standing watch. Lance Corporal Gray snickers in the darkness behind me.

"Relax. That's just some fucking rice farmer taking pot shots in the dark. Does it every night. Must be his personal contribution to the 'cause.' Never hits anything. Nothing to worry about."

Gray is my fire team leader and assistant squad leader. Another short-timer. Been in-country almost ten months. Sandy-haired, skinny twenty-year-old from Arkansas. Married. I like him. Southern "twang" makes me feel at home.

A flare pops high overhead and floats lazily across the river. No sign of the sniper. Relax, huh? Okay. Shit. What, *me* worry? I guess after ten months of this shit I'll get used to it too. That little probe of the lines at Dong Ha a few nights ago has still got me on edge, I guess. How can these guys be so calm? I'm still nervous as hell.

Like that damn ambush our squad went on last night. Moved through the wire just after dark, heading downstream along the river. So damn dark you couldn't see shit. Everybody stuck a white plastic C-ration spoon in the back of their helmet headband so we could see the guy in front of us. Don't know how in the hell the point knew where to go. I guess after a while your eyes must adjust better to this darkness. I sure hope so.

Stumbled along for about half a mile or so and set up our ambush along a trail that follows the river. Laid there for about two hours I guess, and then I saw 'em! Several gooks coming our way, spread out between the trail and the riverbank. I was excited as hell—thought my damn heart was gonna jump right out of my throat.

Picked out one of the figures and waited for the gun team to blow the ambush. And waited . . . and waited . . . Jesus H. Christ, guys, they're getting *awfully* close . . . shit, they're almost on *top* of us now. What the hell's the matter with you assholes? God, they must all be sleeping. Should I shoot? Better wait . . . better blow it now or it may be too late. God, somebody fucking *do something!*

Almost on us now. Flip my safety off and selector to full automatic. Aiming in. Gonna blow *that* fucker away, anyway . . . *shit—where the hell did he go?* Hey, they're *all* gone! Just disappeared. There one second and gone the next. Damn. I *know* I saw 'em. I *think* I did.

Look over at the others in the squad. They're awake, staring into the darkness, looking bored. Oh, *Jesus!* I almost blew the ambush on a bunch of conjured-up shadows! Came *so* fucking close. What a fool I would've felt like. But they *looked* real. . . . As real as the ones at Dong Ha, and I *know* for a fact they were real. God, will I ever get the hang of this shit? I better, before I really fuck up and get myself or somebody else killed.

Standing shirtless atop our squad's hooch, stacking more sandbags on top of our little palace. We "souvenired" us a section of that heavy metal runway from the Seabees for our roof. Adding all the sandbags we can get hold of on top hoping to make it as mortar-proof as possible. Our area is just off the southern end of the airstrip on the river side and is a sitting duck if Charlie decides to throw a serious barrage at the runway.

Been here about a week now, and starting to fit in. Starting to finally get my shit together somewhat. Haven't been fooled by any more shadows since that first ambush. Been on a couple of squad-size patrols. Listening posts every third night. Other nights we each pull two two-hour watches in the bunkers on the line. No action yet, other than a few widely scattered mortar rounds and some pot shots from our resident farmer-sniper. Sounds like a damn weather forecast.

Some guy I haven't seen before is coming from the platoon CP towards our hooch. Humming some sort of country-western song. Good. Must be another southerner.

"This second squad?" No southern drawl there.

"Yeah. Mike Helms, PFC. Glad to meet you." I brush the dirt off and extend my hand.

"Charles Morton. Lance Corporal. Call me Chuck." Strong handshake and a friendly smile.

"Stow your gear inside, Chuck, then grab an E-tool

and help Banks there fill some bags. We'll swap off later."

On watch again in one of the bunkers near the river. Morton cutting Zs on the soggy sand of the bunker's deck. He seems to be an all-right dude. Real happy-go-lucky attitude. Getting to like him a lot. Keeps trying to get me turned on to country music. Sings it all the time. Can't sing worth a shit, but sings it anyway. Wouldn't think a guy from Chicago would like that stuff. Him and Duvall would make a great duet. God, what a racket that would be. Probably make every water buffalo around here di-di.

Quick glance around the area from the light of one of the occasional flares. Nothing moving. Real quiet tonight. Sniper must've decided to take the night off. No mortars at all for two days. Been here a little over two weeks now. Got a few more new hands in the platoon. Feels good not being the FNG. Not an old salt yet by any means, but not the greenest either.

Good, time for Morton's watch. I'm tired. Need to get some sleep. Big day tomorrow. First big operation. Whole company's going. Big sweep through some forest area southwest of Quang Tri City. Probably be some real action. Excited and scared.

Morton takes the watch. I try to sleep . . . toss and turn . . . too damn quiet . . . Loud cracking of our pet sniper's rifle sounds somewhere down the line. A couple of flares pop and sizzle. That's more like it. Drifting off to sleep.

11

We awaken in the predawn darkness to a chilling drizzle. God, it's hard to believe that it can be so cold in this place. All the stories I ever heard about Vietnam were about how damn hot it was—one hundred twenty degrees in the shade and people dropping like flies with heat exhaustion and such shit. Guess that'll come later. For now I'm sandy, wet and cold. Miserable.

Ah, that hits the spot. Banks just brewed up some of his infamous C-ration coffee. You have to stir it real quick or the vile shit tends to dissolve your spoon. Feels good going down, though. Gray declines in favor of some hot chocolate. Smart dude. His mama didn't raise no fool.

I choke down another mouthful of dry pound cake and check over my pack once more. Supposed to be gone for three or four days. Not much to pack. Got an extra skivvy shirt, two pairs of socks and extra M-16 rounds stuffed in the main compartment. In another pair of socks I've stuffed enough cans of C-rats for two or maybe three days, and have them lashed to the top and sides of my pack along with two 60mm mortar rounds. My poncho is rolled and tied to the bottom. Two canteens, bayonet and a battle dressing hang from my web belt (I've gotta scrounge up another canteen or two before the weather turns hot, I've been told). Four fragmentation grenades are crammed in one pocket of my trousers, and two smoke grenades in another. Two bandoliers containing twenty full magazines of M-16 ammo crisscross my chest, bandito-style. I carry a heavy can of M-60 machine gun ammunition slung from a strap over my left shoulder, and my less-than-trusty M-16 rifle in my right hand. All ready to go to war—*if* I can manage to walk with all this shit.

Mid-afternoon. Been humping for hours and have seen nothing. Warmed up some, and the sun has tried to break through the clouds a couple of times. Still a light rain falling, almost continuously. Crossed the river on the outskirts of Quang Tri City early this morning and headed southwest. Been following some half-assed excuse for a cart trail that roughly parallels the river since then. The company is strung out in a slow-moving column, ten meter intervals and staggered on both sides of the trail. Third platoon has the point now; we're in the middle of the column and first platoon has the rear. Thirty or forty meters to either side and near the front lone Marines trudge through the tangled brush and occasional trees, providing security against the column being ambushed from the flanks. We pass by another ornate pagoda standing near the riverbank. Beautiful. Quang Tri Province seems to be a mixture of Buddhism and Catholicism. Seen a few Catholic churches as well as pagodas. Heavy French influence from the old days, I guess. Very pretty and tranquil setting. Hard to believe there's a war going on.

Baboom! Deafening roar of an explosion. Ugly black cloud mushrooming up ahead on the right flank near the river. Evil whining of shrapnel and showers of dirt and debris everywhere. Smell of burnt powder hangs heavy in the thick air. From the ground where I've thrown myself, I stare disbelieving at the body cartwheeling end over end, rising almost to treetop level, now slowly falling back to earth and disappearing again into the vortex of the volcano from which it spewed. Suspended animation . . . slow motion. Can't be real. Desperate cries of *"Corpsman up!"* and shouts from platoon and squad leaders break the unnerving, ringing silence which has engulfed us. Trying to bring order to chaos and confusion. Gotta get a medevac in . . . form a hasty perimeter around a clearing.

Corporal Garcia leads our squad toward the river. Have to pass within a few feet of the blast area. See the body, or what's left of it. Jesus . . . it's Dykes . . . at least I *think* it is. The face is burned, but the fat lips . . . yeah, it's Dykes. There's only the upper torso . . . just one arm. Empty abdominal cavity and ribcage glaring hideously through shredded flak jacket and utility shirt. Eyes open in an unseeing stare . . . blank, painless expression. I tear my eyes away and hurry past, aghast. Can't shake the grisly scene. Feeling sick. Goddamn. Dykes . . . dead. Blown to shit! Christ.

Muffled *wump-wump-wump* growing louder. Chopper approaching. Vintage CH-34 flying low over the river, landing in clearing amid yellow smoke and leaves from rotor wash. Wounded aboard. Lump that was Dykes aboard. Chopper lifts off, banks sharply to the right and disappears around tree-covered bend in the river. Saddle up and move out.

Dug-in for the night atop some nameless, numbered hill. Two men to a hole. Morton hunkered down beneath his poncho against one side, trying to sleep. Rain falling harder, tiny rivulets slowly turning the bottom of our foxhole into a quagmire. Shivering in sopping misery. Maybe I'll catch pneumonia or something and get out of this mess for a while. Warm bed, clean sheets, hot chow. Little things taken for granted all my life. Not so fucking insignificant now. Never gonna take *shit* for granted, ever again.

Didn't eat tonight. Too tired, I guess. Keep seeing Dykes—face all black and staring up at the sky like that. Never did find his lower half. Just disintegrated, I guess. Eighteen years old and gone forever. Gunny Townsend said he must've tripped a booby-trapped arty round, probably a one-five-five. Doesn't really matter what it was. . . . It sure did a number on him. Blew him away, *forever!* Having trouble with that sinking in. Eternity . . . hard concept to comprehend.

Must be close to noon now. Hope we stop soon. Been humping along the river again all morning and my young ass has just about had it. The sun broke through about mid-morning. Starting to finally dry out. Feels good. Boots are still soaked though, squishing water with every step. Feet sore. Hooked up with an ARVN unit early this morning. They're up ahead of the company and a little closer to the river. Good. Let *them* hit the shit first.

Sudden cracking and popping of rifles up ahead . . . oh shit, *here it is!* Double-timing forward across a rutted road, gasping for breath now, more from excitement than exertion. Heavy fire coming from tree line just beyond a big cemetery about two hundred meters ahead. Jesus, firing intensifying quickly! Chattering machine guns and numerous explosions adding to the din. Doesn't sound like M-60s—gotta be gook guns.

Another big burst of firing opens up from across the river to our right. God, rounds are snapping everywhere, and close! Our platoon fans out and faces the river, sprinting for the better protection a slight rise in the ground offers ahead. Wicked hissing, snapping and cracking; leaves, limbs and splintered bark flying from bushes and trees catching rounds meant for us. Ten thousand infuriated hornets seeking to sting the life out of their victims.

The ground shudders as incoming B-40 rockets scream and explode, sending geysers of wet earth and hot shrapnel in all possible directions. Streams of white-hot tracers flying back and forth across the river as our gun teams battle theirs in deadly duels. Hollow *pop* of M-79 rounds from our grenadiers seeking targets in the thickets across the river. Lying prone and popping round after round at a couple of muzzle flashes I've detected in the bushes on the far bank. Getting into this shit . . . not scared . . . blasting away—*get some!*

"*Aww . . . Ouch!*" Black Marine to my right grabbing the side of his neck. Jesus, he must be wounded!

"What is it, man—you hit?" Worried inquiry, looking

for signs of blood spurting from beneath his clutching fingers.

"Shit, no. Your goddamn hot brass is going down my collar and burning the shit out of me!"

"Sorry, man." I crawl ahead and to the left a few feet so my expended shell casings won't land on him. Find my targets and resume firing.

The crescendo from the direction of the cemetery slacks off suddenly. Something's wrong. . . . It sounds all one-sided. *Shit!* The damn ARVN are di-di'ng back this way! They race wild-eyed past us and across the road. Some of them drop into the slight gully of the roadbank and begin firing frantically over our heads in the general direction of the gooks. Others keep going and disappear into the trees beyond the road. Out-fucking-standing! Getting shot at from *three* directions now—the gooks from the cemetery, the gooks from across the river, and the chickenshit idiotic coward sons of bitches ARVN from our rear! Jesus H. Christ—*now* I'm scared.

Behind me I see Captain Langston running with his radioman toward our forward platoon in the direction of the cemetery. A sudden, sickening hollow *thunk!*—not unlike an overripe watermelon bursting open on hard ground—and the RTO spills forward. The CO rolls him over and screams for a corpsman. Doc Poteat is trying to get to them, but the withering fire is too intense. From a few meters away I see frothy, pinkish blood bubble from the stricken grunt's chest with every labored breath. Bad shit . . . sucking chest wound.

Our 60mm mortar crews have finally set up and are giving the gooks across the river hell, walking bursts all over them. The firing abruptly ceases from that direction. *Get some, mortars!* Doc is working on the radioman now and a medevac has been called. Heavy firing continues from the cemetery as our forward platoon continues to do battle with the gooks up there.

We're up and running in that direction, rounds still whizzing and snapping overhead. We gain the edge of the cemetery and spread out, taking cover behind the round earthen burial mounds of the Vietnamese departed. Corporal Garcia screams for me and Morton to cover Doc Hamm and another Marine who are racing forward among the mounds for a wounded gunner. We pop up on either side of the circular grave firing furiously on full automatic. Cram the empty magazine into a pocket and quickly jam another in and keep firing. Gotta keep the gooks' heads down so Doc can do his thing.

Jesus H. Christ! A wall of green tracers flies at us from two directions at the far end of the graveyard. Crossfire! Down we go as great hunks of sod blasted from the mound shower us. Goddamn—that was *close!* Got our young asses zeroed in. Time to vacate this position. We race frantically from opposite sides of the mound and dive headlong behind two others a little farther among the dead. Dark clouds have taken over control of the sky again, and a cold rain begins to pelt us.

Doc Hamm and the Marine are dragging the wounded gunner back to safety. Garcia calls to us to help the A-gunner get the gun team's gear back. Can't leave it for the gooks, I guess. Up and running. Tracers flying again. Evil green eyes seeking to tear my body apart with their piercing stare. Desperate dive behind another mound. Made it!

Where's Morton? Where the fuck is *Morton!* Shit, hope he ain't hit . . . there he is, scrambling like a goddamn crab around the side of the mound where the A-gunner-turned-gunner is. One of our platoons has flanked the gooks, and our mortars are working them over, big time. Return fire dying away . . . stopping. Gooks are hauling ass. *Di-di, motherfuckers!*

More medevacs to carry away our wounded. Nobody KIA—unbelievable! All that shit flying around for what seemed like hours, and nobody dead. Couple of guys real bad off, though. Doc Poteat says they might not make it.

ARVN back up, milling around. Chattering and smiling those stupid smiles. Posing for pictures with gook bodies. Sons of bitches. Supposed to go in hot pursuit after the VC we just whipped. They don't look very-fucking-anxious. I hope they get their sorry, worthless asses waxed.

12

It's been a few days now since Dykes bought it. Exactly how many, I don't know. Real easy to lose track of time over here. The days just sort of seem to run together. I'm not really sure even what day of the week it is.

We're patrolling an area of beautiful rolling hills covered mostly by what looks to be harvestable hay. Scattered hooches of various sizes dot the landscape here and there, and an occasional fencerow breaks the terrain. I guess this is the Vietnamese version of farm houses and barns and other outbuildings. Real pretty scenery. With just a little imagination you'd swear you were out hunting quail on a cool gray autumn day somewhere in the southern United States.

To my left about fifteen or twenty meters away Lance Corporal Gabriel eases cautiously through the golden-brown haygrass and pauses before the latest of several fences we've crossed since early morning. Thick, tangled bramble of vines and briars entwined amongst the strands of wire and encircling the posts. God, what a great place for rabbits! Bet I could hunt this row and kill my limit in a couple of hours. My mind snaps back to reality as Gabriel signals for me to come over to him with a wave of a black arm. A ten-foot section of fence near where he's standing lays nearly flattened against a cushion of briars and brush. Looks like a good place to cross without ripping the shit out of our trousers on the barbed wire which tops the fence.

"Ya see dis shit?" Gabriel asks, lone yellowish front tooth flashing prominently against pink gums and thick dark lips.

"What shit?" I return, seeing nothing out of the ordinary except an old dilapidated fence that's been pushed over.

"Dere, right *dere!*" he says, kneeling down and pointing at the fence.

Jesus! A damn trip wire running inches above the downed fence and disappearing into thick undergrowth on either side. Barely visible. Christ, I would've probably walked right through it. Shit. "What's it leading to?" I ask, fighting the urge to turn and run screaming as far away as I can get.

"Damned if ah know, and ah shore as hell ain't 'bout to go fumblin' through dem bushes to find out. Go tell duh lieutenant what we got."

I hurry back down the column and meet Lieutenant Simpson already working his way up to the front of the platoon to see what the holdup is about. He looks the situation over and confers with Gabriel. Seems to be about as knowledgeable about this shit as I am. Asks Gabriel for a suggestion.

"Well, if it was me, suh," slow, heavy south-Georgia drawl, "Ah'd blow duh shit out of duh muthafucka. Whole goddamn fence line li'ble to be booby-trapped."

"Good idea, Gabriel. Do it." Lieutenant Simpson is green, but he ain't stupid. More than willing to let seasoned grunts handle tight and unfamiliar situations. Good sign in an officer.

Rest of the platoon falls back and takes cover. Gabriel pulls the pins from two frags and chunks them simultaneously into the brush on either side of the tripwire. *"Fi'ah in duh hole!"* he hollers as he hauls ass and jumps into the depression where I've taken cover, about fifteen meters from the fence.

Ba-ba-boom! Three quick explosions rent the air. Booby-trap blown. The platoon passes safely through.

Gabriel has been breaking me in on walking point. Got moved to his fire team in an effort to more evenly distribute the new guys with the salts. Black dude from Georgia. Kinda taken me under his wing like a mother hen and showing me the ropes. A real likeable guy. Starting to get real tight with him. He loves the kids that hang around the perimeter at Ai Tu. Always laughing and joking with 'em, and handing out cake and cookies and cigarettes from his C-rations. The kids all call him "numba one honcho." He's the first splib I've really been friends with since Johnnie Davies from my high school baseball team. That's what we call the blacks—"splibs." Hell, they call us "crackers," or "honkies." Nothing racial about it at all. No slurs intended or taken, either way. Only colors that mean shit in the bush are the green we wear and the red we bleed. There it is.

The concussion hurls me to the ground before I even hear the booming report. I shake my head, trying to clear the cobwebs and rid my ears of this terrible ringing. What the fuck happened? What am I doing down here? *Oh shit—Gabriel!*

Fighting my way through the tangled brush, trying to get to him. Gotta help him. Feeling woozy . . . why won't this ringing stop? What happened? Doc, what happened? Making me sit down, checking me over. No blood. Can't hear very well. Can't think clearly. Bad ache and buzzing in my head. Voices sound far away and strange. Get up and walk over to kneeling figures.

Oh, *Jesus! Gabriel!* He's covered with blood, utilities shredded. Writhing in agony, back and forth, back and forth. *"My ahm . . . my ahm!"* he's screaming. The voice is totally unfamiliar to me. Not like Gabriel to scream and cry. Always laughs and smiles. Maybe I'm dreaming.

Oh, god—his arm! It's *all* fucked up. Big chunks of meat torn away, grisly white bone sticking out in two odd directions . . . barely hanging together. No, no, not Gabriel . . . he's my friend and he's gonna take care of me and teach me how to survive this shit.

Sitting down in the weeds again. Head is starting to clear. Chopper lifting off above whirlwind and disappearing beyond the gray horizon. Thinking how stupid and unfair all this is. I'm daydreaming about hunting rabbits, and he finds the wire. Thirty minutes later he's all fucked up and I'm not even scratched. Hell, he was damn good on point . . . knew his shit.

So much for experience. Looks like Lady Luck plays a big part in this game, too.

* * *

I have officially been christened "Teapot." In one of
those crazy moments where you'll do anything to relieve
the boredom that sets in so often around here, I sang a little nursery school jingle for a couple of the guys in the
squad. They got a big kick out of it and mentioned it to the
lieutenant at a platoon meeting yesterday. Lieutenant
Simpson ordered me to sing it for the entire platoon. I felt
like an idiotic court jester or something, but figured what-
the-fuck—anything for the cause, and did it anyway.

*"I'm a little teapot, short and stout (both hands on
hips), here is my handle (right arm looped, hand on hip),
here is my spout (left arm outward, palm up); when I get
all steamed up I just shout (bouncing up and down), just
tip me over (leaning way over to left side) and pour me
out (bouncing up and down on tiptoes)."*

Jesus, the guys ate it up. Belly laughs and applause. You
talk about being hard up for entertainment—these people
are desperate. Bob Hope I ain't, but I'm glad I did it anyway. Lance Corporal Porter liked it so much he started
calling me "Teapot," and drew a real nice picture of a
whistling kettle on the back of my flak jacket. Another
sign of acceptance into the platoon. Been here only about
a month, but I don't feel like a new guy anymore. One of
them, now.

We got a couple of more new guys in the squad—Lance
Corporal Jack Larson and PFC Gary Beard. They're not
really "new guys." Larson came over from first squad after
Gabriel got wounded, and Beard has been on KP duty at
the Seabee's mess hall since he got here three weeks ago.

He hasn't been in the bush yet, so I guess he does qualify as a new guy. He's a crazy little bastard from Maine, funny as hell. Regular comedian. Always clowning around, keeping us laughing. Good to have around. Strangest sounding accent I've ever heard. I hope he'll do okay in the bush.

Larson's pretty much a salt. Been in-country nearly four months. A veteran of the heavy fighting around Con Thien. Seemed a little snobbish when I first met him, but after a couple of days of getting to know him I changed my mind. He's a first-class dude. Knows his shit in the bush. Big-city boy from just outside New York City. Carries one of only two of the M-14s left in our platoon (crazy Doc Hamm's got the other one). Gung ho as hell.

The other day we were on a platoon-size patrol and started taking fire from a hedgerow across an open field about a hundred meters away. The platoon took cover behind an old brush-covered dike and returned fire. After a couple of minutes, Larson told me to follow him. We worked our way to the end of the dike. He hollered *"Let's go!"* and I found myself following him into the open, completely exposed, firing from the hip like a couple of John Waynes. We emptied our magazines, ducked back behind the dike, reloaded and dashed out, firing again. We did this crazy shit three times, Larson laughing hysterically and me about to piss in my pants the entire time.

After the gooks broke contact and di-di'd, I asked him what the fuck we'd done that for? He just laughed and said these VC rice farmers around here can't hit shit. Not like the hard-core NVA regulars up near the DMZ. Crazy bastard.

* * *

Our squad has the ambush again tonight. Lucky us. Another gut-wrenching stumble in the dark, followed by about eight hours of lying in the bone-chilling dampness trying to stay awake just in case some gooks would happen to wander by. Wonderful entertainment. Not one ambush in the entire company's bagged anything since I've been here. Charlie's evidently got more sense than we do. While we're out shivering and shaking and losing sleep, he's curled up in some warm hooch staying dry and boom-booming mama-san. Shit. At least on perimeter watch we can almost stay dry and get a little sleep. This ambush shit sucks.

We follow the river downstream for a few hundred meters, then turn to the west to Highway One. We follow it northward a ways and again head west across a brushy flat near the railroad tracks. We set-in with half the squad facing the tracks and half facing back toward the direction of the highway.

Corporal Garcia calls the CP on the PRC-25 and tells them the squad's in position. I rub another squirt of bug juice on the back of my neck and ears and stick the bottle back under the black rubber strap which encircles my helmet. Mosquitoes are feasting despite the night's chill. Pull my collar up against the cold. All ready for another night of fun.

A couple of hundred meters to the north glimmers of light from numerous lanterns and cooking fires penetrate the pitch blackness of the dismal night. Good size vill up there. Probably passed through it on patrol before. Yeah, pretty sure we have.

Oh, shit. Somebody must've spotted something. Whispered word being passed down through the squad. I stretch my head over toward Banks and strain my ears.

"Saddle-up and be quiet; we're moving."

I turn and pass the word to Morton. Wonder what the hell's going on? We've only been set-in about an hour. On our feet, heading toward the lights of the village. Making too much noise despite our efforts at silence. God, I hope we're not fixing to make a night assault or something. Wish they'd tell us peons what-the-fuck's going on sometimes. Shit. Even a damn ambush is better than charging through the dark after some gooks that I can't see and don't know where the hell they're at anyway. I don't like this shit one bit.

Getting real close to the vill now. Eyes beginning to pick out shapes in the darkness. Looks like some sort of compound or something. Hey, I know where we're at now—it's the CAP unit. Wasn't the vill I thought it was, but this is better. Fucking-A! Squad of Marines living here with the PFs. Popular Forces are like a neighborhood militia unit. The Marines train 'em and help provide security for the vills around here. Combined Action Platoon, they call it. Winning their hearts and minds and all that shit. Supposed to be number one duty, but I don't want any part of it. I don't trust the little bastards. Be afraid I'd wake up with my throat cut or something.

Garcia pops a green flare in a low arc and we head for the wire. They must be expecting us. Moving through the gate into the compound. Layers of concertina surround the area, and fighting trenches lead from bunker to bunker around the perimeter. Several large tents with wooden sides and floors stand side by side in the center of the camp. Gawking PFs wearing tailored utilities and soft covers grin at us from several of the defensive positions. They look as young and neatly attired as a troop of Boy Scouts. We look like unkempt, raggedy-ass grungy bastards in comparison. Whose goddamn war *is* this, anyway?

Garcia and Gray being greeted with bearhugs and good-natured insults by a burly red-headed Marine. Corporal Evers, their former squad leader. With the company until five months ago. Extended his tour for six months to get CAP duty. When Garcia found out the location of our ambush, he contacted Evers on the CAP's frequency and arranged for us to "sandbag" it for the night. Gonna spend the night in here instead of two hundred meters south where the company thinks we are. Happens all the time, Gray says. Suits the shit out of me.

Sitting on a stool in one of the tents, picking out tunes on a guitar that one of the CAP Marines has. Haven't played in about a year, but the chords are coming back to me and the fingers have quit fumbling somewhat. Getting mellow on a couple of cold beers. Can you beat that shit? Cold beer! We get a warm one once every couple of weeks, but these guys have *cold* beer. Out-fucking-standing! This CAP unit shit ain't all that bad, after all. Might think about it myself, later on.

Been playing some Beatles, Byrds, and Rolling Stones. Threw in a little Dylan, Donovan, and Peter, Paul and Mary for good measure. Regular "sing along with Mikey." Just about used up my whole repertoire. Used to know a lot more, but can't remember them all now. Even appeased Morton with a half-assed rendition of "Your Cheating Heart," "Fraulein," and "Knoxville Girl." Some of the chord changes didn't quite fit, but he didn't notice and loved it anyway. His voice ain't one bit better with accompaniment. Brought the house down with my famous version of the Animals' "House of the Rising Sun." Ruined my voice on that one and had to quit singing. Not sure whether the applause and cheers were for my artistic ability or the fact that I finally had to shut up and let the others sing. Oh well, nothing another cold beer won't cure.

Get to sleep the whole wonderful night on a cot with a blanket and pillow! Can't believe this shit. Haven't been this comfortable since I've been in-country. Socks, boots, flak jacket—all off. Sleeping in just our trousers, snuggled in blankets, warm and dry. No ambush; no LP; no perimeter watch. Just sleep.

Startled awake by the loud popping of rifle fire and the booming of explosions! What the fuck is going on? Where am I? Oh, yeah, the ambush . . . the CAP compound.

"Get the fuck up! Get out of here! Get to the fucking wire!"

Jesus, Evers is screaming at us like a raving banshee. Fumbling in the dark for my rifle. Jam a couple of frags into a pocket, grab a bandolier, and I'm out of the hootch racing blindly for a trench, still not fully awake. The hum and whine of nearby rounds flying overhead quickly wipes the sleep from my eyes. Jesus! Red tracers incoming. Guns! I thought those fuckers used green tracers.

Into the trench, weapon loaded, returning fire at unseen targets. Only two frags. I had six . . . can't worry about it now, but if they get in the wire . . .

Oh, shit. Mortars. *Incoming!*
Crumphh! Crumphh!

Each sickening explosion followed by high-pitched humming of shrapnel seeking nocturnal targets. Flares from the 81s at our base camp popping overhead now, shedding light on the foray. No visible targets that I can detect . . . keep firing into the shadows.

We stay on the line until dawn. Dreams of a good night's sleep shot to shit. Luckily for us nobody in the squad was hit. A couple of PFs slightly wounded. CP called during the probe and told us to be aware of the activity and to intercept the gooks if they passed our way. Garcia did a good job of bullshitting us out of this one. Damn lucky we didn't get found out and hung up by the balls for not being where we were supposed to be. If anybody had got hit, we would've been up Shit Creek for sure.

Seems like we can't get a goddamn huss over here, no matter what we do.

13

Humping it again on another two or three day company-size sweep. Our platoon left the main column early this afternoon, crossed a small stream and have been trudging our way up and down an endless series of brush-covered hills and gullies ever since. Goddamn can of gun ammo's just about to kick my young ass. And these frigging mortar rounds I've got strapped to my pack—shit—lotta good they're gonna do us. Mortars stayed with the company. Feel like ditching the bastards.

Zing-crack! Platoon flattens out; heads popping out from above low bushes like prairie dogs, looking for signs of sniper. Another round and report. Hell, he's way off, wherever he is. Hear the damn rounds singing before the rifle fire. Lieutenant Simpson and Staff Sergeant Chalmers scanning the surrounding hills with binoculars. Nothing. Reporting incident to the CO. Moving out again.

Another several hundred meters and we're down again. Two quick shots, much closer this time. Excited shouting from first squad up ahead on point. Two gooks sighted on a hill to our right front, hauling-ass down the other side, about three hundred meters away. Oh Jesus, Lieutenant, be reasonable . . . shit! Platoon double-timing for the hill where the gooks were sighted. Can hardly walk with all this shit I'm humping and Mr. Gung Ho Ninety-Day Wonder has us trying to run down the bastards in a foot race. Man, let the fuckers go . . . too tired for this shit.

We reach the base of the hill and skirt around the left side. Still running. Lungs are screaming for oxygen, leg muscles burning and starting to disobey command from brain to keep pumping. Goddamn can of gun ammo wreaking havoc on my upper thigh. Lieutenant Simpson beginning to take on all the attributes of Staff Sergeant Burns in my mind . . . cursing him for all I'm worth. Can't keep this shit up much longer.

Don't have to. Quick succession of shots has us sprawled again. *Damn* close this time! Muzzle flashes from a small hill seventy-five meters to our front and we're all scrambling for better cover. Platoon returning fire, but the gooks are di-di'ng again . . . see two disappearing over the crest. I'm starting to get a bad feeling about all this. Fuckers ain't playing cat and mouse just for the hell of it. Bet my beer ration they're trying to sucker our asses into a big-time ambush.

The Lieutenant went to school for this shit. Ought to have it figured out by now. He's conferring with Chalmers and the squad leaders. Good. They'll talk him out of this crazy shit. Get our young asses headed far, far away from this place most skosh.

Simpson's on the horn again with the Skipper. Jesus

H. Christ! Word is to get on-line and sweep the hill. I do not fucking *believe* this idiotic bullshit. Oh man, we are gonna get zapped. We are gonna get fucking zapped. I don't like this shit, I don't like it at all not even one little bit. . . . Almost to the top now. Full automatic. Cold, sick feeling in my stomach. Just waiting for it . . . walking right into the shit . . . I know it's coming, I know it's coming, I can feel it, I don't wanna be here, anywhere but here.

We reach the top. . . . No ambush. Sickening tension eases just a bit. *Whew!* Man, I thought for sure we were gonna catch hell up—

Ka-Ka-Ka-Ka-Ka-Ka-Ka! Burst from automatic weapon sends me reeling to the ground. Christ Almighty! Almost took my fucking head off. Frantically crawling for cover—any cover. Not a whole lot to choose from. The fire is coming from yet another hill beyond this one, about the same height. Only reason we're alive. If it was any higher our poor asses would be in a real sling. Most of the rounds are passing just overhead. The firing's not as intense as I thought it would be after that opening burst . . . must just be a few of 'em over there.

Oh, god! I suddenly grow cold all over and begin to shake uncontrollably. . . . Fifteen feet ahead of me, under the same group of bushes where I've sought refuge, lays a fearsome-looking artillery shell with a thin black cord leading from it down the far side of the hill. Command detonation! I turn and try to holler a warning, but my tongue won't form the words and my vocal chords have ceased to function. I am absolutely paralyzed with fear. I've been scared many times, but this is beyond that type

of fear. Horrible Death stares me in the face. The gruesome round has become the Grim Reaper and leers
hideously at me. He speaks to me in a macabre voice,
telling me he's going to do to me what he did to Dykes. I
can't tear my eyes away from the hypnotic stare by which
I'm transfixed. . . . I am a dead man.

"Off the hill! Get off this fucking hill!" The squad leaders are screaming, gesturing feverishly for us to fall back
beyond the crest to the safety of the slope. Somebody else
saw it too . . . that's good. Gotta get out of here but my
body doesn't seem to want to work anymore. Sharp blow
to the top of my helmet. It's Larson. Tells me we gotta
move fast. Struggling up and sprinting for the slope but it
feels like I'm in slow motion . . . taking forever to get
there . . . never gonna make it. Gonna be just like Dykes—
an over-done piece of meat.

Down the slope in near panic. Platoon racing for the
protection of a ravine to our right. Stopping there, counting heads, getting organized. No more firing from the
gooks. Regaining my senses. Sick to my stomach again.
Lieutenant Simpson calling for an arty strike of the gook
position. Whistling overhead. Sharp explosions two hills
away. Moving out the way we came.

Half dug in for the night on another hill, a cold rain
falling. Ground so rocky I could barely dig deep enough to
curl up like a fetus and be below the surface. Good anal-
ogy—fetuses curled up seeking protection in the womb of
Mother Earth. Not much comfort here. Lying in the mud
and shivering from the cold.

Almost bought it big-time today. Wonder why they

didn't blow it? Bad wire? Faulty cap? Something saved our asses. Or Someone . . . So damn tired. Gotta try to sleep before my watch. I shift to my other side and pull my poncho tighter around my neck and shoulders. Body heat finally beginning to take the chill off the puddle in which I lie. Fatigue overcoming visions of Dykes. Drifting off into restless slumber.

Hooked back up with the rest of the company this morning. Heading east. Terrain changing from brushy hills and valleys, becoming almost flat with scattered tree lines and occasional rice paddies. Our platoon's in the middle for now. Company CP group moving with us. Better than the point, but small reward for almost dying yesterday. Forward observer sticking to the Skipper and his RTO like glue. Clean utilities, boots, helmet cover. Fresh from the States. Must be his first op. How 'bout that shit. I gotta whole month on him.

Rifle fire cracking from the tree line on the far side of the rice paddy we've been trying to skirt by balancing on a narrow dike. Oh, christ—not again! Shit. Every goddamn day now it seems like . . . into the murky water, using the dike for cover. Shit! Son-of-a-bitching worthless piece of plastic shit is jammed again. I dunk my '16 into the slimy paddy water and swirl it around. It's worked before, hope it does this time. Back up and firing. Six rounds and it jams again. Damn fouled-up piece of worthless trash! How the hell do they expect you to fight a goddamn war if they can't even give you a weapon that works half the time? Shit!

Weapon cleared again and firing. FO talking excitedly

on the horn . . . all-fucking-right! Calling in the big shit. Naval gunfire. Gonna blow those gooks into oblivion.

Loud, air-sucking whistle coming in. Getting closer . . . louder. Jesus, sounds like a goddamn freight train roaring out of the sky. Louder and louder, almost deafening . . . enormous, bone-jarring explosion less than fifty meters away. Flash hurts my eyes, shock wave knocks me damn near silly. Terrible screaming of huge shrapnel flying all around us. Another explosion and another and another and the rice paddy has become a horrible maelstrom! Oh, Jesus—they're short they're short christ almighty *they're short they've called 'em in right on top of us!*

The Captain and the FO are frantically trying to raise the ship on the net to adjust the coordinates. The huge shells continue to fall among us and we've become mud worms, pressing ourselves deeper and deeper into the oozing muck, seeking fervently for a semblance of safety in the quagmire.

"Stop it stop it goddammit stop it!" PFC Huggins, a new black dude in third squad is standing up and shaking his fist at the sky, temporarily gone berserk. Another Marine nearby tackles him and drags him below the surface as another mammoth round erupts in showers of water, mud and shrapnel.

Oh god oh god oh god! The air is torn with an awful tornado-like guttural whirring as an enormous jagged missile hurtles invisibly toward me louder and louder and louder and *kawhunk!* The dike behind which I lie cringing reverberates with the shock of the huge fragment as it slams into the spongy earth directly in front of me. Showers of mud and water cascade down upon me and steam rises in a dreadful hiss like an evil geyser from the pits of Hell.

The shelling stops as quickly as it began. The tree line is silent. Gooks must've hauled ass when the first round came in. Squad and platoon leaders checking for casualties . . . another miracle. Nobody even wounded. Water and soft muck of the rice paddy absorbed much of the destructive power of the big shells. Can't believe I'm still alive and in one piece. Can't hack much more of this shit. Gotta have a break. Shaking all over again. Two days in a row now I've looked Death right in the face and walked away from it. Jesus H. Christ, my insides are a quivering bowl of Jell-O. I can't take this shit much longer. One month down . . . god, only one month.

On perimeter watch again, and thankful for it. Feel safe and secure here. Not like the bush. When I first got here this base camp seemed so desolate and foreboding; now it almost feels like home. Not exactly like being in your living room flopped out in front of the television with your feet propped up, but it sure beats the hell out of Indian Country.

Sharing the watch with PFC Wayne Warner, a tall, lanky, pimply-faced Texan. Newest of the new guys. Ten guys in the squad now; about as many as you can hope for over here. I've been here just over a month and I've got more time in-country than five of the guys in our squad. A pretty green bunch, but we've seen some shit the past couple of weeks. No cherries left, anyway.

Flare pops high over the river. Shimmering light reveals the shadowy form of a pagoda two hundred meters downstream. Larson's got an LP out somewhere near there. Got Beard and Browning with him. Browning—funny name for him. He's a blond-haired bespectacled kid from Ohio, with the palest skin I've ever seen except maybe that mulatto maid one of my paper route customers had years ago. Loves horses and rodeos and all that cowboy shit. We call him "Hopalong"—"Hoppy" for short. He fired damn near two-forty on qualification day at Parris Island, so the Lieutenant's letting him use one of the Starlight scopes the platoon was issued.

Hoppy's been volunteering for every damn LP for nearly two weeks now. Gonna get himself a gook, he says. Starlight scope lets you see pretty good at night, unless it's absolutely pitch black, which it almost always seems to be. Strange, eerie greenish world when you look through the thing. Sniper activity has picked up lately. Our old sniper's either honed-up his shooting ability or somebody else has joined the game. Plugged a Seabee through the shoulder the other evening near dusk, and there's been several near-misses. Skipper wants that gook greased.

Another real quiet night. Just like I like it. No mortars for a few days, and the sniper hasn't checked in yet this evening. Pleasant change from the terrible fear and tenseness I've felt over the last few days. God, I think I must've aged ten years during that last op.

Got a new set of utilities this morning. Well, not new, but clean and dry. My old trousers had become more like a skirt since I ripped them up on the fence lines the day Gabriel got hit. Walking through a damn little vill near the outskirts of Quang Tri City and having the girls and mama-sans pointing and giggling at me . . . shit. Embarrassed as hell. Big bad American Marine with his family jewels flapping in the breeze. Got a needle and thread from Doc Hamm and tried sewing them up, but I can't sew worth a shit and they kept reverting back to an olive-drab kilt. Sure glad to get another set. Besides, after a month they were getting a little ripe anyway.

Amber glow interrupts the night as another flare floats lazily beneath its chute. To the southeast a sharp red tongue darts from the black sky and flickers back and forth across the earth like an evil serpent sensing its surroundings. Get some, Puff! Big, bad gun ship. Puff the Magic Dragon. Can chew up every square inch of a football field in a matter of seconds when he works out with those six-barreled miniguns. Bad motherfucker. Real glad he's on our side.

Tiny flecks of red and green arc erratically low over the horizon. Distant firefight. Far away. No sound. Reminds me of colored sparklers I played with as a kid. Red and green. Christmas colors.

Christmas! Hey, it's only three or four days away, I think. Have to find out from somebody tomorrow. Care packages from home oughta start getting here any day. Oughta be good ones, being Christmas and all. This will be the first Christmas I've ever been away from home. Do it right if you're gonna do it—all the way on the other side of the world! Wonder if Santa Claus delivers over here. Shit. Forgot to write my letter. Probably too late now:

Dear Santa, All I want for Christmas is for this shit to end so we can go home soon. How about tomorrow? Well, you probably can't fill that order,

Santa, so how about an M-14 to fight this fucking war with? At least then I'll be reasonably sure that when I squeeze the trigger it will go "bang" instead of "click" like my old rifle does. I've been a real good boy this year, Santa. I've been obeying my orders and I always eat every bite of my ham and mother-fuckers. Clean my can, every time. Well, I know you're real busy packing your sleigh and feeding your reindeer and all that shit, so I'll close for now. Love, Mikey. P.S.—I'll leave some C-ration cookies and purple Kool-Aid outside the bunker for you in case you're hungry. Keep your head down and your ass covered!

Loud *pop!* of an M-16 startles me awake. Single round. Wonder if Hoppy—

"I got him! I got him! I got him!"

Jesus H. Christ! Crazy bastard's yelling at the top of his lungs. Supposed to be a damn listening post, for christ sakes. Voice is carrying over the entire area. Better di-di their young asses back inside the wire, most skosh.

So, ol' Hoppy got the sniper. Out-fucking-standing— *get some, Hoppy!* Wonder if it was our resident sniper or some new guy? Slight twinge of sadness. Gonna kinda miss having the old fucker around, if it was him.

14

Christmas Eve. *Deck the halls with boughs of holly. 'Tis the season to be jolly. Keep an eye out for ol' Charlie, fa la la la la, la la la la!*

Damned if the platoon didn't get stuck with a holiday hump today. Been at it since dawn. Being extra cautious—nobody wants to die on Christmas Eve. That would tend to put a damper on one's holiday spirit. Besides, there's a big turkey dinner with all the trimmings waiting for us back as the Seabees' mess hall this evening. Moving real slow, staying off the main trails, avoiding contact at all costs.

Headed west this morning. Supposed to make a big arc through the countryside and come back in from the south. Slow and easy. Checkpoint to checkpoint. Rice paddies have given way to lush forests dotted here and there by isolated clusters of small hooches and what looks like vegetable gardens. Indigents busily tending their small fields, paying us no mind as they work their hoes methodically. Small flocks of multicolored chickens scatter at our approach, their scratching and pecking momentarily interrupted by green giants. An occasional pig that could never hope to place in the county fair looks up at us unconcernedly with squinty eyes and muddy snout and resumes rooting. Tiny toddlers, clad only in thin pullover shirts, peer at us from the shadows of doorways and the folds of mama-san's baggy pants where they cling for protection. Wide, inquisitive dark eyes dominate their otherwise blank little faces.

We break for chow at a deserted farmstead. Thatched roof of the hootch partially caved-in. Unkempt fields overtaken by weeds. Pens and fences strangled with groping vines. Wonder where these fuckers went? Probably out humping it for ol' Uncle Ho.

I reach into one of the side pockets of my utility shirt and pull out a can of Chef Boyardee ravioli. No C-rats today. Fucking-A. That shit's been shelved until the goodies from our care packages run out. Everybody in the squad's received at least one in the last few days from family back home. Items from the real World. Cherished novelties from the past. Cans of Spam, ham, tuna, vegetables, fruits, juices, soups, chili, Vienna sausages, potted meat, sardines. Packs of presweetened Kool-Aid of every flavor, jars of Tang, instant coffee, and hot sauce. Hooray for hot sauce! Boxes of cookies. Packs of candy bars, chewing gum, Lifesavers. Homemade cakes and cookies reduced to crumbs by the perilous journey to the far side of the planet. Eat 'em anyway, and enjoy!

Larson got extra boxes of the assorted cheeses his mother always sends. Beard got a bunch of delicious red juicy apples from his folks up in Maine. Share and share alike is the rule. Everybody gets something from everybody else's treasure. Nobody hordes and nobody wants. There it is.

Extra plus for the squad in my package. The family sent a little artificial Christmas tree and some tiny ornaments, most of which survived the best efforts of the mail clerks who seem intent that no package arrive undamaged. We decorated it last night and set it up on a crate in a corner of our hooch. A nice touch. Helped us get into the spirit of the season somewhat. Morton sang "Jingle Bells" and a couple of other songs, and got us to join in. Not exactly the Mormon Tabernacle Choir, but it did help ease the homesickness we've all been feeling lately.

Somebody found a well out behind the hooch. Good. Give us a chance to dump this oily, foul-tasting shit we got from the water bulls and get some decent water for a change. I help Morton and Thompson gather our squad's canteens and head for the well. Would you look at this shit. Like a picture out of a story book. Three-foot high circular wall fashioned from crude mud and straw bricks; gabled roof perched on four stout posts and covered with thin tiled shingles; wooden bucket tied to rope curled around windlass and crank. Looks like a damn wishing well. Wish I had a coin. I'd toss it in and wish me the fuck out of here!

I look down into the well. Shit. Leaves, cigarette butts and other assorted trash floating placidly on the surface. What the fuck, it's gotta be better than that diesel fuel we've been drinking. Christ, even Kool-Aid can't disguise that horrid shit. Just hope nobody's pissed in here lately. I draw a bucketful, scoop the crud off the top and fill the canteens. Doc Poteat stands nearby in his grandfatherly way and reminds us to be sure to use our Halazone tablets. Sure, Doc . . . fuck it. At least if I catch the shits or something I might skate out of the bush for a couple of days.

Mid-afternoon and we're still at it. Nothing's happened and feeling good about that. Don't know what the hell they've got us humping out here for, anyway. Thought there was supposed to be a two-day cease-fire in effect. Guess the brass wants to let Charlie know we're on our toes in case he wants to start some shit. Out-fucking-standing. Who's gonna tell the booby-traps and mines they're not supposed to blow up because there's a cease-fire on? Goddamn worthless know-it-all sons of bitches. Won't catch *their* sorry asses out here humping the boonies. Oh, no, the brass is too good for this shit.

Terrain has changed again. Lot of rice paddies. We avoid some and cross others warily. Cloud cover has broken up. Gray sky has given way to brilliant rare blue. Beautiful against the greenery of the landscape. Never seen so many shades of green as there are over here. Green so green that it's almost black. Green so pale that it's practically translucent. And every shade of green imaginable in between. This is definitely one beautiful country, most affirmed. Beautiful and deadly. Like the sirens who lured Sinbad's sailors to their doom in those flicks back home on Saturday mornings. Fuckers thought they were gonna get their rocks off with the beautiful sea nymphs. Wound up getting their shit greased *on* the rocks, instead. This place is like that. Luring, lovely, and lethal.

* * *

Late afternoon. Sun showing signs of retiring for the day. Clouds rolling in from the east off the sea, pulling their gray blanket across the retreating blue sky. Nice while it lasted. Gotta be getting close now. Couldn't be more than a couple of klicks left. I can almost smell the turkey.

Walking tail-end-Charlie with Morton, covering the platoon's rear. There's that sound again . . . like bells ringing in the distance. Reminds me of the steeple on the First Baptist Church back home, chiming that pretty Westminster melody and then bonging out the hour for the whole city to hear. Damn, that makes me homesick. Christmas Eve. Shit. Wish I was home.

Ringing's getting louder. Starting to pick out scattered but distinctive notes during lulls in the gusting wind. Sounds vaguely familiar somehow . . . Christmas carols . . . that's it—I'm hearing Christmas carols! Wonder where it's coming from?

Gotta be real close to the outskirts of Quang Tri City now . . . almost home. Turkey and dressing and gravy and hot rolls and butter and cranberry sauce and pumpkin pie and no war for a day. There, up ahead. A Catholic church. Gray stuccoed front, shaped something like the Alamo. I *knew* I wasn't imagining it. No bell tower visible. Wonder how . . . hey, that's it. They're playing recorded music over loudspeakers! "Silent Night." They're playing "Silent Night." I'll be damned—Christmas carols ringing out over the Vietnamese countryside.

We pass within seventy-five meters of the church, then angle to the left up a gradual slope. I look over at Morton, a few yards to my left and rear. "How about *that* shit,

Chuck? Don't that beat anything you ever saw, hearing 'Silent Night' in a place like—"

Sudden burst of automatic weapons erupts behind us. Cold fist slams my guts, chilling fear racing up and down my spine. Dreaded hissing and snapping of hot invisible messengers of death filling my world again. *Oh god oh god!* Sprinting madly for the crest of the slope . . . not gonna make it, Chuck, we're not gonna make it.

Rest of platoon over and returning fire at the gooks who are set-in behind a hedgerow paralleling the church. Legs turning to mush . . . too far away, too far away. Ground behind us exploding in showers of clods as automatic weapons seek us out. Going down, going down, gotta go down—too hot too hot.

Sprawled on the ground, rifle and helmet tumbling away. *Oh Jesus, oh god!* Lone tree between me and Morton being denuded of bark, turning into a million toothpick-sized splinters . . . *stay down, Chuck, don't move!* . . . no chance but to lie here and play dead. Ground still churning around us, air above thick with sickening whines . . . fingers clawing the earth in fear and desperation. Consciously squeezing my rectum tighter and tighter against the round I know that any second is going to tear through my asshole and rip its way through my body and blow out the top of my head. . . . Platoon pouring a fusillade of fire back at the gooks. Rounds still popping and cracking and laughing and taunting and kicking us with dirt in our terror and humiliation.

It stops . . . contact broken. Gooks have di-di'd. I lie there cringing, afraid to move, amazed I'm still alive. I look over at Morton. There is a sick, tormented glaze in his eyes. I know I am looking into a mirror. I want to puke. I need to shit. I want to run away from this nightmare, turn the corner and be home. . . . *Cease-fire, my ass!*

We struggle to our feet and gather our rifles and helmets and what's left of our sanity and scramble up the slope to the waiting platoon.

"Man, we thought y'all was dead!" says Johnson, a new black dude from first squad.

"We did too, man. We did too."

We hurry on into the deepening shadows. Turkey dinner's gonna be good . . . hope I can eat.

"Silent Night" fades in the distance.

15

On board choppers and heading for Con Thien. "The Hill of Angels," missionaries from long ago dubbed it. Screw that. Any angels around there done got their shit blown away by the NVA. Nothing angelic about that place. "The Meatgrinder," the grunts call it. Very descriptive. The battalion got its ass chewed up good around there in September and October. Con Thien is one bad motherhumper.

The crew chief-door gunner motions to Corporal Garcia and yells something into his ear through a cupped hand against the cacophony that reverberates within the metallic hull of the grasshopper-looking CH-34. Garcia nods his head, a grim look on his usually emotionless face. Shit. He's had that look ever since coming back from the squad leaders' meeting last night and giving us the word. Gray and Larson got it too when he told us where the company was going. They're the only three left in the squad who were up there before. They look like someone who's been rescued from shark-infested waters, allowed to rest aboard ship awhile, and then told they've got to swim back to shore. Like a cruel joke. I think we may be in for a world of shit.

The word from the crew chief is being passed from ear-to-ear through the squad. I strain my senses trying to hear what Banks is yelling to me amid the din of the roaring chopper. I don't think I heard him right, so I holler for him to repeat what he just said.

" . . . incoming . . . can't land . . . have to jump . . . "

Jump? *Jump? My ass!* What the fuck do they think we are, a bunch of paratroopers or something? This ain't no parachute I'm humping. How the hell do they expect us to—

A sudden lurch to the right and we are in a steep, sweeping dive. *Oh Jesus, we're falling.* I want off this son of a bitch! I hate roller coasters and Ferris wheels and I sure as shit hate helicopters and we must be crashing.

The chopper levels off somewhat. The crew chief signals to Garcia and he finds his feet and motions for us to stand up. Out of the door I can see red earth flashing by and growing closer and closer. Garcia screams at us to get ready. . . . Oh christ, I'm scared . . . we're going way too fast to even *think* about jumping out of this flying fiasco and we must be a hundred feet up and I know I'm gonna break my fucking neck.

Another violent bank to the right and now this son of a bitch is damn near flying on its side! Oh god, *here we go*— Garcia's out and Gray and Beard and Warner and Banks and *oh shit I'm next* I grab my rifle in one hand and the can of gun ammo in the other and Jesus it looks like an awful long ways down and so fast and *oh fuck.* . . .

I hit the red clay muck and roll like I've seen paratroopers do in the movies, aware of the shrill whistles and explosions of incoming artillery before I complete the less-than-coordinated imitation. Most of the squad is up and scrambling for a nearby trench and I pull myself and the can of ammo from the sucking mud and plod after them as fast as the reddish-glob monster will allow.

Into the trench I go with a half-stumble and half-dive as another shell screams in and suddenly I'm laughing hysterically from relief and fear and Larson and Banks and Beard are laughing with me. We look like a bunch of kids who've spent the day having mudfights, and we sit in the oozing shit pointing at each other and laughing contagiously while Death rains from the sky in a vain attempt to seek us out and destroy us. I think we all must be going crazy.

Saddled up and moving out, heading south. The incoming lasted only a few minutes, not real heavy. Just one of Charlie's regularly scheduled harassments, according to Larson. No big deal. Yeah, right. Shit, these guys really caught hell up here a couple of months ago. Thousands of rounds. What scares the shit out of me doesn't seem to even faze them. They've seen so much that their emotions are calloused over, I guess. Mine still seem to be real tender to the touch. Guess I'll harden in time. I'd better.

The sky is clearing a little, and the warmth from the peeking sun feels good against my mud-plastered utilities. The road we're humping down is oddly dry, and the trampling of so many boots causes little swirls of red dust to rise and disappear with the wind. Damn choppers must've dumped our asses in the only mudhole left at Con Thien.

Gently undulating brush-covered hills dominate the terrain on both sides of the red gash down which we travel. Occasional hedgerows and clusters of small stunted trees enhance the beauty and danger of the landscape. Jesus . . . Ambush City. Marines from several battalions fought all summer to keep this pitiful stretch of road open between Con Thien and Cam Lo. Seems unreal to be walking peacefully through the scene of what was so much carnage just a few months ago.

Clouding up again. High overhead, air-sucking sizzles mark the path of friendly artillery as it hurtles through the overcast toward the north. Distant muffled popping and cracking from the east—somebody's in the shit. Sounds like the popcorn machine at the movie theater. I close my eyes and try to envision the sights and smells of the crowded lobby on Saturday mornings. Man, that would be good right now—a big tub of popcorn dripping with butter and a box of Goobers and a large Coke filled with slushy ice, *mmm-mmm*. It doesn't work. Shit. I can't even remember what popcorn smells like. How can I forget something like that so soon? Damn C-rations have done fucked up my sense of taste and smell, I guess.

Crossing a small bridge over a low gully through which an unobtrusive stream meanders. Numerous bunkers manned by waving Marines extend in every direction on both sides of the road and stream. The Washout. Bastards' Bridge. This is where the battalion got hit so bad just a couple of weeks before I joined 'em. Golf Company got overrun and the gooks even hit the battalion CP hard. Battalion CO wounded; XO dead. Golf Company CO and three platoon leaders KIA. Hand-to-hand, hot and heavy. Jesus. Chills crawl up and down my spine as I stare fascinated at the scenery of what was for Two-Four a bloodbath just two months ago. The peaceful little stream was then a raging torrent and the battalion had defended the bridge site against superior numbers of NVA forces trying to cut the supply route north to Con Thien. The Marines had kicked ass when it was all over, but at a terrible price. No wonder Garcia and the others looked strange when they heard we were coming back up here. A sick feeling of envy comes over me. I think I wish I could've been here with them. If only I'd been sent over a few weeks earlier . . . I wonder how I would've reacted? Would I've measured up? Stop it, stupid! Better be damn glad you weren't here, you damn idiot. Better hope you see no more shit at all for the rest of your tour and go home alive. Beats the shit out of going home in a body bag, no matter how much you've been through. Can't tell any war stories from six feet under.

Midday now, and it's getting hot. The sun's broken out again, and from its zenith beckons rivulets of sweat from beneath my helmet which flow down and are swallowed up by my once green but now reddish-brown utilities. Hottest I've been since I got here. Christ, I can hardly wait until summer. My sopping feet cry out in protest with every squishing step from within my sauna bath boots. I dread the thought of pulling off my socks after this op. White, rotted between-the-toes flesh enmeshed as one with the fabric of my socks. Corpsman snipping away the socks and meat to expose deep bloody cracks. Fighting back tears as he paints the violated area with that shit that's not sup-posed to burn but feels like he just set my feet on fire. Fun,

fun. Doesn't take long for trench foot or jungle rot to set in over here.

Left the road just south of the bridge and heading west. Hedgerow after hedgerow, separated by brushy grass-covered fields. Isolated abandoned paddies here and there, protected by thick tangled tree lines.

Firing erupts ahead, and the lieutenant yells for us to get on-line. Garcia leads our squad in a sprint to the left and we tie in with the other two squads of our platoon behind some low grassy mounds that may have once been a continual dike in better years. Rounds are snapping and buzzing around us. I duck my head a couple of inches and squint my eyes and tighten my shoulders, as if doing so will help ward off the whizzing death-darts flying toward us at several thousand feet-per-second. I can't see a damn thing, not even muzzle flashes, but they must be in that hedgerow about two hundred meters away.

The shit's getting heavier. Several machine guns join the foray, rattling away. Light show of green and red tracers crisscrossing the clearing between us. Our 60mm mortars are walking in among them now, but these bastards aren't breaking off. Shit! A few rocket rounds land nearby, off target for now. Pick a bush and fire away. Muzzle flash in the shadows at the base of the thick hedgerow. A target. Jam another magazine in and crank 'em off at the spot. Steady, controlled fire. Picking out several flashes now . . . the company's pouring it on. Goddamn, these bastards are *still* not moving. Our rocket teams are blasting the shit out of the hedgerow, but those hard-core mothers are answering back with RPGs and the battle is growing and growing. Cries of

"Corpsman up!" coming from down the line. Shit, somebody's hit.

We must've gained fire superiority in our sector; incoming rounds have slacked off considerably. Unless . . . oh shit, I hope the bastards aren't trying to flank us!

From out of nowhere a Phantom swoops down from the sky and over the enemy's hedgerow like a bloodthirsty hawk in a chicken yard. *Grrrrr! Grrrrr!* With a terrible growl the F-4's 20mm guns rip the length of the gooks' position, sending showers of limbs and leaves in all directions like a hedge-trimmer gone wild. Steep arcing climb and the roaring engine overpowers the staccato of the firefight. Another bird racing suddenly to the attack . . . watching in awe as a big cigar-shaped cylinder tumbles erratically from beneath the jet and erupts in an inferno of orange flame and black smoke. Heatwave smacks us in the face as the jellied gasoline does its fearsome duty.

First Phantom screaming back to the assault, dropping another load of hellfire onto the hapless gooks. *Kawoosh!* Roaring firestorm racing the length of the already blackened, ravaged hedgerow. Jesus-fucking-Christ—*get some, Phantoms!*

Unreal calm broken only by the sizzling and crackling of burning brush from the dying hedgerow. No gunfire at all from either side. Gooks must all be dead. Nobody could've possibly lived through that shit. Son-of-a-bitching Marine pilots have got balls bigger than grapefruits! Both Phantoms passing incredibly low in front of our position. For an awful second, terror grips me as I think they might be making a pass on us. Hurtling across our front now, tipping their wings slightly one way, then the other. Pilots staring at us through their canopies. Smiling and giving a "thumbs-up." We stare back, mouths agape. Frantic waving and returned gestures all along the line. Dumbstruck, like kids meeting their matinee idol heroes. Damn, what a show!

Another soaking, shivering, sleepless fun-filled night in the Nam. Dug in somewhere just below the DMZ. Our fourth day out . . . or is it the fifth? God, I'm miserable. So damn cold. Sitting under my poncho in the steady rain just behind our hole keeping watch. Watch? Ha, that's a laugh! With this rain beating down I can't hear a damn thing, and it's so dark I can't even see my hand in front of my face. That's no bullshit. Might as well be deaf and blind. Fucking gooks could be sitting on the other side of this hole and I'd never know it. Shit. Too tired to care anymore. At least if Charlie puts one between my running lights I won't be wet and cold and tired anymore. Just dead. Won't know it, anyway.

Acrid smell of stale cigarette smoke and burning C-4 fumes waft upward through the downpour and attack my nose and throat. Morton and Beard are hunkered down in our hole, covered with a poncho in a vain attempt to keep warm. Soft, reddish glow of their cigarettes, barely visible in the blackness beneath the pitiful shelter, suddenly drowned out by the harsh glare as they ignite another piece of plastic explosive. Greenish-white light rushes from under the rubber poncho and dances up the muddy walls of the foxhole. Muffled sounds of hacking, choking coughs. Jesus H. Christ! The idiots must've lit half a bar of that shit. Probably looks like a goddamn volcano from a distance. Hope the gooks ain't looking this way.

Stomach's growling again. Started out on this op with only two days' rations. No resupply yet. Choppers won't fly in this shit except for emergency medevacs. Nothing at all to eat the last two days except that little tin of peanut butter me and Beard finished up tonight. Cut the shit out of my little finger trying to scrape up the last bit. Oh well, at least I probably won't have to crap for a few days anyway. It's hell trying to wipe your ass with soggy shit paper. Thought we had it made when we found those banana trees this morning. Damn things were green and harder than a honeymoon hard-on. Managed to cut a few open and tried to eat 'em. Jesus! Turned our mouths inside-out like a mouthful of unripe persimmons. Gotta get my mind off of food, think about something else for a while. . . .

Like that area we went through yesterday. Dead. Best way I can think of to describe it. That place, that piece of the Earth, was dead. Absolutely. Completely. Like being in the Twilight Zone. Enormous bomb craters everywhere I looked. Hundreds of 'em, maybe thousands. Our whole damn platoon got in one for a briefing and there was more than enough room for everyone to spread out and avoid bunching up. Had to be fifty feet across and twenty feet deep. Maybe deeper. Bottom was filled with water. Outside the craters for hundreds of meters in every direction bleakness and desolation reigned. Unreal landscape of earthen red and death-pallor gray. Occasional blackened, splintered tree trunks standing in defiant death like ghostly sentinels above the desecration. In this land of such greenness there was no green at all. None. Strange.

Unsettling. An eerie, heavy stillness hung over the place. No natural sounds. No animals, no birds. Not even an insect. Arc-light did a real number on that place. Those B-52s pounded it into oblivion. Killed it. Must be what the surface of the moon looks like. Real glad to get the hell away from there.

I strain my eyes at the luminous dial of Morton's watch. Shit, almost 0200. Supposed to've woke Beard up an hour ago. Ah, fuck it. Just as soon be wet and miserable up here as down there in that stinking mudhole. Let the bastard sleep, if he can. I ain't all that tired anyway. Guess I can hack it for a couple of more—

My head snaps back as I awaken suddenly. Damn. Fucking fell asleep. Mixture of fear and relief rushes through me, replacing my fatigue. My heart pounds as I think of what could've happened. Way to go, Mikey. Get yourself and everybody else killed because you can't keep your sorry ass awake! Shit.

Alert now . . . something's different. Hey, the rain has stopped. I suddenly realize I can see a lot better than before. I can make out the distinctive shapes of trees and bushes, and their shadows wavering in the light breeze. Shadows? I glance at the sky. Stars . . . the moon. I haven't seen a clear night since . . . hey. Resupply! Choppers will probably fly out in the morning. Out-fucking-standing! I think I've got a sudden craving for ham and motherfuckers. Almost makes my mouth water just thinking about it. *Mmm, mmm.*

I reach into the hole, pull back one side of the poncho and grab a shoulder. "Hey, Beard," I whisper, "wake up. Your watch, man."

Beard struggles to extract his muddy ass from the muck and props down grumpily beside me. I tap him on the leg and point to the sparkling heavens. He looks up and smiles.

Motherfucking shit-eating ball-busting Green Machine bastards! We've got the LP tonight. Shit. Suicide City. What a totally screwed-up day, and now to top it off me and Morton and Beard and Thompson get to take a pleasant little stroll outside our lines and play hide-and-seek with about a thousand fucking NVA tonight.

Started the morning off with a bang, dodging short-rounds from our 60mm mortars. Fucked up faulty charges or something damn near waxed our own asses. Bad enough Charlie slings all kinds of shit at us. Now we get to have fun and games with our own fucked up ordinance falling in our laps. Couple of guys from weapons and third platoon medevacked out. No KIAs, luckily. Mickey Mouse shit they give us to fight with. Half the goddamn M-16s are reliably unreliable, and now we can't trust our own mortars. Wonder what they'll come up with next?

We hit the shit again today around mid-afternoon. Another duel from hedgerow to hedgerow across another abandoned paddy. Threw everything the company had at the bastards, but it was a Mexican standoff until we called in a couple of Huey gun ships. Worked 'em over real good with their guns and rockets. Larson was right—damn NVA up here are good, most affirmed. Hard-core motherfuckers.

They finally broke contact, and we followed 'em into a heavily forested area full of cart trails crisscrossed with secondary trails and footpaths. Jesus H. Christ, you talk about a clusterfuck! Confusion City. The company split into platoons which split into squads which split into fire teams which split into lost grunts wandering every-which-way down dozens of trails through brush and trees so thick you couldn't see five feet into the mess. Contact between friendlies strictly by word of mouth:

"Hey, Hoppy, is that you over there to my right?"

"Teapot? Yeah, it's me and Thompson. Where the fuck is everybody else?"

"Should be to my left. Heard Gray and Warner over there a minute ago. Said to keep contact and stay on-line."

It got to be a real interesting game. Hear a noise or see movement, drop down and challenge it in your most authoritative, scared shitless voice. If it doesn't answer, shoot the shit out of it. Worse than running through the North Carolina pinewoods playing those gung-ho war games and shooting blanks during ITR. Constant yelling; sporadic bursts of rifle fire and occasional booming of frags interspersed now and then with sustained firefights when somebody stumbled into the real shit. A total fucking SNAFU.

Toward dark I had to cross a main trail to hook back up with the rest of the squad. How I wound up on the other side of that trail from the others I have no idea. No recollection of crossing it before, but there I was. It was a beautiful area. Tall trees bordering both sides, their tops growing together in a protective canopy. Reminiscent of a shady lane leading to a stately antebellum plantation home in the Old South. Got about halfway across when a gun opened up about fifty meters up the trail. Flicking red tongue of flame spitting red tracers at me. Did my best imitation of a track star across the expanding trail and dove headlong for the safety of the brush on the far side. Sharp pain beneath my left eye. Blood. *Jesus, I'm hit!* No. Shit, jabbed a sharp stick in my cheek when I dove. Skated again. Not by much, though.

Company somehow managed to find all of its scattered pieces, got coordinated and dug in for the night in a fairly open area near the junction of two big trails. Medevac came in the fading twilight and took out a few casualties and three prisoners third platoon captured. One of 'em was a fucking broad. Didn't know the NVA had any women. Might be a nurse, or maybe there's some VC regulars in this shit, too. Sitting in our shallow holes choking down some Cs when Garcia gives us the word about the LP. Shit, there went my appetite. Hunger replaced by a bellyful of fear. That's our ass. This fucking place is crawling with gooks, everywhere. Shit.

Moving out now. Heading down one of the trails. Some old gook fighting holes are supposed to be on either side of the trail, about a hundred and fifty meters out. Jesus. I remember the gun that almost greased me just before we set in for the night. That was a whole lot closer than a hundred and fifty meters. The gooks have gotta be everywhere between here and there. Wish we could sandbag this one, but there's nowhere to go. Don't know what they need LPs out here for. Shit, they *know* where the gooks are—*every-fucking-where!* Wonder why the CO never leads an ambush or LP?

Fuck this shit. Probably gonna get blown away on this one. Wish I had the guts to say I refuse to go on this stupid worthless idiotic bullshit LP. Too chickenshit to do that. At least we've got four guys instead of the usual three. Almost half a squad. Sounds better than just an LP.

The night is clear again. Stars are out playing their timeless twinkling games, and the moon is on the rise. Visibility is good. Don't know whether to be glad or terrified about that.

The trail narrows and we find the holes located in the shadowed fringes of the brush on either side. Good concealment from anyone coming up or down the trail, and an excellent view both ways. Me and Morton ease into adjacent holes on the left side of the trail, while Thompson and Beard find two on the right about twenty feet away. Morton straightens the pins from a couple of frags and lays them on the edge of his hole. I'm humping the radio and I ain't about to take it off like we usually do. Screw that. Even though there's four of us, it's gonna be a hundred percent alert all night long. Two looking one way down the trail, and two looking the other. Fear has defeated our fatigue.

Almost midnight. Moon has passed its apex and started its slow slide toward the west. Steady breeze from the northeast blows shadowy imps from the trees to dance flittingly upon the moonlit trail. Four weary sets of eyes stare hard into the night in constant vigil, trying to distinguish fantasy from reality. Pulses surging with every creaking vine against branch and rustle of leaves. My mouth is dry and my back aches from the burden of the radio. Should've took the damn thing off, I guess. Too late now. Make too much movement and commotion in this clear night. Can't risk it.

Barely audible sit-rep request from the CP. I key the handset twice to indicate everything is okay. . . . Yeah, hunky-fucking-dory, except we're out here in the middle of gookville and every minute has to be taking ten years off our lives but that doesn't really matter because we're probably gonna die out here before the night is over so what-the-fuck difference does it make, anyway? Shit.

Morton grabs my arm and squeezes tight. "I think I hear voices!" Excited, fearful whisper.

Oh Jesus, no Chuck. You don't hear anything. It's just your damn imagination running away with you I'm sure but I'm not really sure because god I think I hear it too *oh shit!*

We look across the trail and now we *are* sure because Thompson and Beard are staring at us with saucer-eyes full of fear and pointing down the trail. The sound is getting louder and more distinct. High pitched, rising and falling, almost musical. Gook voices. No mistaking that sound. Oh, christ. Hey, maybe they're ARVNs . . . not supposed to be any in the area. But if they're gooks, what-the-fuck are they doing diddy-bopping down this trail, chattering like they're on a Sunday picnic or something, for christ sakes? They must know where we're at. Doesn't make any sense, but there's no time to be philosophical about it now because several of those dancing imps have turned into real live gooks walking down the trail toward us and they're only about fifty meters away oh shit should I call in the movement or not or what because they might hear me but maybe I should alert the company or—

Morton snaps me out of my self-induced panic with a flurry of sign language. He's gonna throw the frags and

I'm gonna fire my rifle full automatic when the gooks get close. Close? They're *already* too fucking close for me and getting closer. Yeah, okay. Oh shit. Jesus, I want to just run away now and forget this awful game because it's no fun anymore at all. Somehow we make Beard and Thompson understand what's up and they're gonna do the same thing from their side of the trail. We'll key on Morton.

I decide to call in the movement so the company will be aware when we blow it. Shit. I can't remember our call sign. Fuck formality. I key the mike and whisper that we've got movement to our front and we may be coming in fast. My voice is broken and choked with fear and the CP requests that I "Say again," but there's no time now because the gooks are only maybe twenty meters away and Morton is starting to make his move and it looks like about twelve or fifteen gooks and their weapons are mostly slung and they're still talking and somebody laughs or at least it sounds like it and Morton arcs a grenade high overhead and Beard does the same and before the first ones land they've thrown their second and I'm up and spraying a full magazine into their midst and I think Thompson's doing the same and god we can't miss they're so close almost point-blank and the grenades are blowing and they scatter and scream and we are up and out of our holes before they can recover and are racing down the trail for our lines and I'm screaming *"LP coming in! LP coming in!"* into the mike so the CP can alert the lines but the gunfire and grenades and my screaming voice have already alerted them and we cover the hundred and fifty meters to our sanctuary in what must be record time but it takes forever and god I hope they don't shoot us coming in please please don't shoot us and we're all screaming *"LP coming in!"* over and over and suddenly we're through the lines and collapsing to the ground and gasping desperately for breath. . . .

We report the action to Lieutenant Simpson and Captain Langston. Good job. Well done.

Company on one hundred percent alert until morning. Except for us. We get to sleep. Ample reward for saving our own young asses. . . . Curled up under my poncho, staring at the winking stars . . . thoughts of home, friends, being safe. . . . Drifting away.

16

The sunrise is incredibly beautiful as it bathes the big island of Luzon with a kaleidoscope of color. Shadowed black hills rise gently from the shore, rolling inland and ever-upward to become lofty green peaks reaching a mile or more into the rosy sky. Reddish-gold ribbon from the emerging fireball sparkle-dances across the placid sea, painting the gray hull of the ship's bow a bright amber. A cool refreshing breeze flows from the east, as if pushed ahead by the advancing dawn. The shrill cry of gulls riding early thermals in growing spirals adds to the spell of the moment. Peace and tranquility.

Got up before reveille this morning and came up on deck to catch this. A couple of swabbies told me and Beard about it last night after chow. Said it would be well worth it if the weather was right. They weren't bullshitting. Beard's gonna wish he'd seen this. Couldn't get him up this morning. Victim of an all-night poker game and a smuggled bottle of rum. Lost his ass to the squids.

Damn. Wish I had a camera. Two months in Vietnam

and I haven't seen anything this pretty. Maybe never in my whole life. Been to the Smoky Mountains before, but this is prettier. I could kick myself in the ass for not having a camera. Beard's got one, but he tells me last night he's out of film. Seems like everybody in the whole damn platoon who's got a camera shot up all their film on the trip over, and the ship's PX was closed. Just my luck. Gotta get me a camera and a bunch of film before we leave Subic Bay.

The sun climbs higher and the shadows retreat a little farther up the slopes of the distant hills. A pale blue haze replaces the pink glow along the eastern horizon. This is our fourth day at sea. We got the word that the battalion was going "on-float" shortly after we got back to Ai Tu from that op around Con Thien. Out-fucking-standing! Skate City. Word is that being the Battalion Landing Team is number one duty. Live aboard ship with the squids. Hot showers, great chow. A real rack to sleep in. Make a landing once every blue moon to act as a blocking force or sweep an area. Stay out in the bush for a few days, and then it's back aboard ship for maybe weeks at a time. A chance to live clean, fat and lazy for maybe five or six months. Shit, by the time we go off-float I'll almost be short! Fucking-A. I'll hafta reach up to tie my bootlaces. Suits me just Jim Dandy. I've had enough of this grunt shit for a while.

The company loaded up on several big six-by's the morning of 2 January and convoyed up to Dong Ha for embarkation. First, the entire battalion gathered on board the helicopter carrier USS *Iwo Jima* for a short but somber ceremony to remember and honor Two-Four's dead from the past few months. Mixed emotions. Sadness and pain for friends blown-away mingled with relief that *my* name wasn't on the honored roll call. Better them than me, I guess.

After the ceremony our company left the *Iwo Jima* and boarded the USS *Cleveland,* an amphibious tractor transport. Humped our seabags, packs and weapons up the gangplank. Saluted the colors; saluted the officer-of-the-deck. Welcomed aboard by the captain and crew. These swabbies are all-right dudes. Platoons and squads split up and guided to our quarters by a resident petty officer "overseer." Banged the shit out of my forehead forgetting to duck as we passed through one of the hatchways along the maze of corridors. This shipboard shit will take some getting used to.

Each squad is assigned separate sleeping quarters, a small cubicle with webbed-canvas stretched across metal framed racks stacked like pancakes on either bulkhead. Rather crude but efficient, and to us grunts, luxurious. Our resident pet petty officer then showed us the head and adjoining shower stalls and explained to us how to take a "Navy shower":

"Wet yourself down quickly and turn off the water. Lather your entire body thoroughly, then quickly rinse and turn off the water again. The idea here, men, is to save water. It must be conserved in this manner to provide for the comfort of the entire ship's crew. Is that understood?"

Yeah, right swabby. We gotcha. Even us dumbass grunts can do that. Wet-lather-rinse. Got it. After weeks and weeks of being filthy, scudsy motherfuckers and wearing the same clothes and not taking our boots off for days at a time and our only shower being the cold rain while we sat ass-deep in mud, we will be sure to *wet-lather-rinse*. Right. Fucking-A, we will.

I gaze out across the expanse of the South China Sea. With the growing light the water takes on a blue-green color. There is barely a ripple to disrupt the almost glassy surface. Sharp contrast to the rough seas we had the past two days. I start back toward the stern and the wide-open deck area the company will be using for formation and PT in another few minutes. Damn, Captain Langston is a real stickler for PT. Had us running laps around the deck during those heavy seas the other day. The ship rose and fell so violently that the deck actually fell out from beneath our feet, and we found ourselves pumping our legs in mid air, then slammed down hard as gravity reintroduced us to the ship's deck. A couple of badly sprained ankles and several skinned knees and elbows and irate corpsmen finally convinced the Skipper to cut us some slack.

Couldn't believe our luck when we found out we were heading to the Philippines for the ships to refit and resupply. Probably be there for a week or ten days. Probably get some liberty too, at least on base at Subic Bay. How about that shit? Just over two months in-country and already getting what almost amounts to an R&R! And then several months of cruising up and down the coast of Vietnam as a standby force, living high-on-the-hog with the swabbies. Somebody up there must be smiling on us. Finally getting a huss.

R&R, my ass! Fucking CO's idea of R&R is to run our asses ragged humping up and down these goddamn mountains. Shit. Gung ho bastard. Object of this Philippine fiasco is to fuck over the troops. Petty-ass stateside-style inspections and boot camp haircuts and spit-shine your fucking mud-stained jungle boots and get all the goddamn rust off your Matty-Mattel M-16 and pick up cig-arette butts and sweep and swab the Quonset hut barracks and run for endless miles and do PT forever and fuck this petty-ass bullshit! I think I'm starting to miss the bush. Beautiful damn country, though.

Saturday afternoon. Me, Morton, Beard and Larson are walking along the recreational beach area of Subic Bay, taking advantage of a base liberty. To our left, a short dis-tance inland among a shady grove of trees, several pavil-ion-covered picnic tables are busily occupied by military personnel and their families. A white sandy beach stretches along the shoreline for a few hundred yards before yielding to a thick growth of trees and tangled bushes growing right to the water's edge. They must've cleared this strip and hauled in the sand. Nice, but sure as hell not as pretty as the beaches back home.

Children of various ages and races play happily in the sand, building castles and making cakes and pies with their colorful buckets and shovels. Others frolic merrily in the shallows, laughing and splashing each other with showers of water that sparkle in the bright sunlight. One persistent boy about six-years-old keeps trying vainly to catch little fiddler crabs that dash across the sand only to disappear teasingly into the safety of their holes inches from his grasping fingers. Patient little bastard.

It's nice to see kids being kids again. Almost forgotten what that's like. The kids in Vietnam don't seem to ever play, at least not the ones I've been in contact with. All they seem to do is beg for "chop chop" or "cigalettes" or stare at you with that faraway blank gaze. It's good to see kids laughing and running and splashing and throwing sand and even fighting over who's got whose bucket. No fear of war, or hunger, or numbness to life in their eyes. Just happy, everyday children. God, I'd almost forgotten they existed.

Numerous sun worshipers lie scattered about the area on blankets or colorful towels, soaking up the hot rays of the early afternoon sun. Several unattached beauties spotted and scoped out. Jesus, those bikinis hardly cover anything! Pangs of passion-hunger well up inside. *Mmm, mmm.* Man, that stuff almost makes my mouth water. The lucky bastards that are stationed here have got it fucking made, most affirmed.

Morton ambles over to where three browning beauties are lying together and puts his big-city Midwestern make on them. Odd man out. Walking back this way, alone. Shot down. What-the-fuck did you do to charm 'em so, Chuck? Serenade 'em with "Your Cheatin' Heart" or something? Must've been your breath or jungle rot. Ah, fuck 'em. Word must be out to stay away from the Marines off the ships. Ain't seen one damn grunt score yet today. Act like we've all got leprosy or something. I guess our short haircuts and our pale legs and torsos make us stick out like sore thumbs. Cut off faded olive-drab utilities-turned-bathing trunks can't be helping our image as surf studs, either. Screw it. They're all probably riddled with the galloping clap anyway, and who the hell needs that? Sure would be nice, though.

* * *

I drain a final swallow from my latest beer and carefully place the can atop the rapidly growing pyramid that covers our squad's table. The noise inside the smoke-filled enlisted men's club is deafening, the whooping and hollering of what seems like half our battalion drowning out the instruments and voices of the Filipino rock and roll band on stage. Corporal Garcia reaches out a long brown arm and grabs the tiny barmaid around the waist and hugs her tightly to him.

"Miss barmaid, another round of beers for my squad. Best damn squad in the best damn platoon in the best damn company in the best damn battalion in the whole damn Marine Corps!"

Ten drunken grunts explode into cheers and "fucking-As." Throughout the huge club other small units of Marines dutifully empty beers and add to their own growing tabletop structures. The race to the ceiling is on. An occasional metallic crash sends clanging cans spinning and rolling in every direction, signally an untimely demise caused by a careless or inebriated hand. Here and there a Marine stands up and makes a solemn toast in remembrance of a fallen buddy, temporarily quelling the roar of the crowd. On the far side of the club, the resident naval enlisted personnel gawk at us like we are some kind of animals who should be in cages in a zoo; they keep to themselves, talking in subdued tones.

Goddamn, we are blowing the steam off tonight! May as well, a lot of us won't ever have another chance. Gonna get blown away KIA. There it is! I ain't *never* gonna survive another ten months of this shit. Not if it's like what

I've been through already. No damn way. Im-fucking-possible. Been too damn lucky so far. Fucking booby-trapped arty round and naval gunfire and damned ambush on Christmas Eve. Shit. I shouldn't be here already. Look at Dykes. Poor bastard didn't last a month. Blown to shit. Bet he didn't weigh fifty pounds. . . .

Merry Christmas, Mr. and Mrs. Dykes. Here's your boy, home for the holidays. Well, part of him, anyway. Couldn't quite find the rest. Happy fucking New Year.

Shit. And I'm supposed to last another ten months? No damn way. Drink me another beer on that thought. I know, I know, I'm gonna be sicker than shit tomorrow. Me and several hundred others. Fuck it. Tomorrow's Sunday and I can sit on my ass all I want to. This might be my last chance to ever get drunk and hung over again. Why cheat myself out of feelings I may never feel again? Eternity's a long damn time to sober up in, so what the fuck?

Clang! Clang! Clang! Corporal Armistead, a burly gunner from weapons platoon, is standing atop a table at the edge of the narrow aisle separating us Marines from the indigenous swabbies. He drops the two serving trays he used as cymbals and grabs a pitcher of beer from one of the Marines seated around him.

"Listen up men, and you swabbies, too. A toast to one of the baddest motherfuckers who ever walked the face of the earth. He had balls that even King Kong would be envious of. More lettuce on his chest than a migrant farm workers' convention. A legend among legends, a man among men, a Marine among Marines. Let us drink to the honor of . . . *Chesty Puller!*"

Stupendous roar as every Marine not already passed out

springs to his feet, cheering and drinking in honor of one of the greatest heroes in Marine Corps history. Chaotic celebrating goes on for several minutes, gradually giving way to a shouting match between Armistead and his buddies and a group of sailors who refused to stand and are mouthing insults in reference to our beloved Chesty's family heritage. With the bellowing roar of a wounded bull, Armistead dives from the table across the buffer zone and lands squarely in the midst of the offending squids, sending tables and chairs and swabbies tumbling in all directions.

In a flash, a wall of green rushes like a tidal wave upon a white beach as Marines swarm into the naval personnel to defend their fellow Marines and honor. We jump to our feet and rush to join the foray, sending our table and four-foot high skyscraper tumbling in clattering destruction.

Flying fists, knees, forearms, hammerlocks, bear hugs, choke holds; pushing, shoving, grappling; chairs and tables and beer cans and I'm punching and somebody blindsides me and I'm on the deck under a pile of bodies and shit it's getting hard to breathe down here and—

Shrilling blasts from the shore patrol's whistles and we're breaking contact and hauling ass out the side entrance and racing down the paved street and onto the dirt street and back to our company area. Bloody noses and busted lips and bruises and skinned knuckles lend testimony to the fierceness of the hand-to-hand struggle. Fucking swabbies. Good thing the SPs showed up when they did, or we would've killed every last one of the mothers.

Ol' crazy Doc Hamm's working his way through the

squadbay, cleaning up cuts and checking us out. Saw ol'
Doc taking on three or four squids at one time. One out-
fucking-standing Marine, Doc is. Got that shit straight.
Ten squids wouldn't make a decent pimple on ol' Doc's
ass. Lot of damn nerve the Navy's got, calling our gutsy
corpsmen "naval personnel." Asshole Navy. Our docs are
as good as Marines as ever humped the boonies. There it
is! Oh, my aching head. . . .

The chopper sets down in the haven of a flat grassy
meadow that makes a small break in the rugged terrain of
a thickly jungled ridge line. The ramp lowers and out we
go at a trot through the galelike rotor wash of the twin-
prop CH-46 Sea Knight. About fifty meters away, at the far
edge of the clearing, the green hulk of a downed Huey lies
almost hidden among the tall grasses and deepening shadows of the waning day. Nightfall comes quickly in these
mountains.

The grounded crew emerge from the direction of their
disabled bird, and with friendly waves and good-natured
taunts take our place aboard the idling Sea Knight. The
big chopper lifts off amid the roar of engines and wind-
storm of blades and disappears into the twilight toward
the southeast. I look around our surroundings. Christ.
We're sure as shit isolated up here on this mountaintop.
Nothing but rugged jungle expanse for as far as I can see
in any direction, and the promise of an inky-black night.
Glad this ain't the Nam.

We drop our gear in the clearing the Sea Knight used
for its LZ and begin clearing rocks and brush from what
will be our bivouac. Garcia sends Hoppy, Warner and

Thompson to gather wood for a campfire, and takes the rest of us on a reconnoiter of the meadow and downed chopper before we lose the light completely. Not much here. The area is roughly the size and shape of a football field. Scattered boulders of various shapes and sizes lie haphazardly about the meadow floor. Clumps of bushes and low gnarled trees hide in the shadows, already beginning to take on the ghostly appearances that black nights always give them. A spooky fucking place, but our bonfire will fix that. And, we don't have to worry about Charlie taking us out. Shit, this is just like camping out back home. Quit worrying. So damn used to being in constant danger I can't even relax and enjoy myself.

First time I've seen a Huey up close. Looks a lot bigger than I thought it would be. No M-60s, no rocket pods. Shit, this thing's practically stripped. Looks almost harmless from here. Not like they do when they're working Charlie over. One bad motherhumper, then.

Fucking flyboys have got it made in the shade. No humping the boonies; no sleeping in the mud and rain. Just fly around, blowing away ants on the ground, then back to the club for cold beer and a warm, dry rack. Can't beat that shit. A real world of hurt if you get shot down, though. That's one advantage of being a grunt—not so far to fall if you get hit.

The warmth from the blazing fire feels good against the chilly mountain air. We sit around the burning logs in a rough semicircle, laughing and bullshitting like a bunch of Boy Scouts on a camping jamboree. Word came down to the company this afternoon that a chopper had made an emergency landing due to some mechanical failure, and that a squad was needed to secure the area and guard the chopper for the night. Garcia sweet-talked Lieutenant Simpson into volunteering our squad for the duty. Good opportunity for us to skate out of the petty-ass Mickey Mouse bullshit for a while. Just a camp out in the mountains with nobody to fuck with us for a couple of days. They issued each of us enough Cs for two days, and one magazine of ammo. Garcia's got his blooper and a few rounds, plus several flares and smoke grenades to distribute among the squad. No frags or claymores or LAWs, but what the fuck? This is the Philippines, not Vietnam. Gotta keep reminding myself of that.

Wonder who we're supposed to be guarding this thing from, anyway? Saw nothing but dense jungle on the flight over here. Maybe some monkeys or rock apes or something. Oh well, never look a gift horse up the ass. We only have to pull a one-hour watch apiece, tonight. Can you believe that shit? Just stay awake for sixty short minutes and keep the fire going. No straining our eyes and ears and asshole trying to find Charlie creeping among the shadows. Just feed the fire and make sure somebody doesn't walk off with the Huey. Fat chance of that happening.

A sudden snapping of twigs and we're rolling away from the fire, grabbing our weapons. Bolts slam home before we remember that our one magazine apiece is in our pockets. Shit. Mumbled curses fill the night as we find our magazines and seat them home with a symphony of metallic clicks. Twenty eyes strain the darkness, frantically trying to overcome the glare of the campfire which has suddenly changed from warm friend to dreaded foe.

Maybe it's just an animal or the wind broke a dead branch off a tree or . . . Speculations vanish as a shadowy figure looms from the darkness and stands silently at the fringe of dancing light cast by the fire. Pulses race and fingers tighten as yet another apparition and then another and another materialize from the blackness and join the first specter in the wavering glow.

Jesus H. Christ—what is this shit? On the top of a mountain in the middle of the jungle . . . Got the drop on us and our asses in a sling, but this ain't the Nam it's the Philippines but who the fuck are they anyway?

"Hey, GIs, you want whiskey?"

The voice is childlike and energetic, and the English is surprisingly good. Walking toward us now. Cold fear washing away as the light of our campfire reveals the smiling faces of four young Filipinos. They appear to be about ten or twelve years old. One may be a little older. Hard to tell about these Asians.

See 'em better now. The three boys have hair something like the Beatles. The girl's hair is long and straight and jet-black, like Cher's. Very pretty. They're dressed like kids from the World would be. What are they doing way the fuck out here in the middle of nowhere?

They tell us their village is only about a mile from here, down the other side of the ridge, and that sailors and soldiers often stop along the road which runs near their vill to buy food and whiskey and souvenirs and would we please like to buy some whiskey, very cheap?

What the fuck? Okay, what've you got? The tallest boy trots back into the shadows and reappears carrying a cardboard box. Inside are several bottles of "spirits." Some faintly resemble the brown of bourbon. Others range from yellow to clear. A couple are a sort of greenish color. No labels. Definitely the products of some local mountain moonshiner.

"Is this shit any good?" Morton asks, in his usual tactful manner.

The young Filipino stares back, feigning hurt feelings as if his integrity has been offended. He reaches in the box and twists the top off a bottle filled with what looks like horse piss, then downs a big slug. He wipes his lips with the back of a hand and grins. "Very good shit!"

We argue a little and haggle a lot, and finally pool what little money we have along with several meals of C-rats. We choose a couple of bottles of each color except the green. Ain't about to touch that shit. Looks like what I puked up all day after that night in Tijuana.

The four youthful entrepreneurs bid us farewell and disappear into the night. We sit back again, relaxed around the glowing embers and break out our booty. Beard takes a sip from a bottle of the yellow stuff, grimaces and hands me the bottle. I look at the bottle hesitantly, then back at Beard. Ah, fuck it. That little shit just can't handle the hard stuff. I down a big swig— *Jesus H. Christ! Ooh!* Burns like hell. Tastes like a cross between butterscotch and kerosene . . . not too bad, though, after it gets down. Mmm, the next few swallows are a lot better. Pretty damn good shit. Everybody else seems to be enjoying it, too. I try the other flavors, but it all burns the same and boy we are feeling really good now, laughing and joking and I love all these sorry-ass bastards and I throw another couple of logs on the fire whose fucking watch is it anyway and I'm getting kinda

tired now so I think I'll just rest for a little while y'all
wake me up when it's my watch. . . .

Our last night at Subic Bay and I've got the duty in our
platoon area. Nothing much to it. Just answer the phone
in the office if it rings, and walk up and down the squadbay
now and then to make sure nobody fucks with anything.

Wasn't my turn for the duty, but I've been feeling kinda
sick to my stomach for a couple of days and I've got the
shits, so I volunteered to take Larson's place so he could
have a final fling with a Filipino filly he met at the PX.
Thanked me profusely, said he owed me one and that he'd
bring me proof of his conquest. Jesus, you'd thought I
saved his life or something. I don't mind . . . don't feel
worth a shit and can't really afford to stray too far from the
head. Probably crap all over myself if I went.

Oh-two-hundred now, and the guys are starting to find
their way back to the Quonset hut by twos and threes.
They stumble and stagger down the squadbay in varying
stages of drunkenness, searching for their racks through
bloodshot eyes and foggy minds.

Here comes Morton and Beard, struggling along, dragging Larson between them. His arms are slung over their
shoulders, mouth hanging open, drool running down his
chin. The eyes are half open, but unfocused. His lips aren't
moving, but he seems to be mumbling or humming, or
maybe he's moaning. Man, is he fucked-up! Looks like the
poor bastard really had fun. He's gonna feel like shit for
the next couple of days, and we're going back aboard ship
tomorrow. Christ, I feel for the poor dude. All that rocking
and rolling . . . Puke City.

I walk over to help Morton and Beard with their cumbersome burden. These two bastards aren't much better off. Ugh! Nauseous smell of soured booze and foul breath threatens to make my already agitated stomach wretch in protest. I turn my face away, take a deep breath and grab Larson's feet. Beard and Morton each grab an arm and we dump him on a bottom rack. Larson groans and rolls over on his side, revealing what appears to be a brightly colored scarf wrapped around his neck. Gotta check this shit out. I lean down to investigate. Son of a bitch. It's not a scarf—it's a pair of bikini panties! Bright purple. How about that shit—the sorry bastard scored. Out-fucking-standing. Get some, Larson!

"Parker . . . Parker . . . Oh god, Parker!"

Screaming, sobbing outburst jolts me out of a sound sleep. Crying and moaning and mumbling, then shouting the name again:

"Parker! No! Parker, goddammit, no!"

Jesus, it's Larson! I swing off the top bunk and race to his rack. Garcia and Gray are already there, trying to calm him down. They're shaking him gently, talking to him, telling him it's okay, but he keeps hollering *"Parker!"* in that terrible, haunted voice.

Jesus H. Christ—shut-him-the-fuck-up, somebody! The voice is scary, unreal, like from another world. Giving me the chills. Like a voice from the dead. I can't stand this shit.

Parker was Larson's best buddy. Been together since boot camp. He took a sniper round through the head while they were on a routine patrol, just before I joined the company. Blew his brains out, literally. I heard that

Larson nearly went ape-shit for a while. Maybe that's why he gets so gung ho and does crazy shit sometimes.

Finally got him calmed down. I lie on my rack and stare into the darkness. A peaceful silence now, broken only by faraway snoring and the wind blowing off the sea and whistling playfully through the window frames of the old Quonset hut. Thinking about tomorrow and the next ten months. Back aboard ship. Back to the war. Just starting to get used to not being afraid all the time, and now we're going back. Don't know if I can hack it again. I get so damn totally scared when the shit starts, all that metal flying through the air trying to tear me apart. Fear's doing a good job. Haven't been hit yet, and that's a miracle in itself. But my insides feel like they've been scrambled. Ah, fuck it. Hey, we're on-float, remember? Shit, we'll probably skate for a few months. Might even come back here again. And by the time we go off-float I'll be a short-timer, and maybe we'll get base security somewhere or something. Might not be too bad at all. Hell, the war could end by then, anyway.

I've gotta get some sleep. Reveille's only a couple of hours away, and we've got a big day ahead of us tomorrow. Yeah. Clean the barracks for a white-glove inspection. Stand around for hours in formation while we "hurry up and wait" for the brass to decide how best to fuck us over. Back to the ship. Salute the colors, salute the Officer of the Deck. Sail back to the war. Stem the tide of communism. Liberate the oppressed people for democracy. Die for your country and the free world. Yeah. Wonderful future.

17

The big iron monster growls and rumbles as it lumbers slowly down the flooded well deck of the USS *Cleveland* and falls ungainly into the choppy sea. A multitude of revengeful oaths and curses fills the sardine-can atmosphere as the violent lurching of the amphibious tractor turns it momentarily into a human pinball machine. Epitaphs drowned out by the roaring diesel as several pissed-off Marines grope in the dim light for lost helmets while others pick themselves off the wet metal deck and flop angrily back down on the benches lining the bulkheads.

Son of a bitch! Einstein wasn't lying when he said "for every action there is an equal reaction," or some such shit. A miracle nobody broke their neck. Shit. Oh well, it beats crawling over the side of the ship down those flopping cargo nets like we did in training back at Lejeune. Now, that's some *real* excitement.

Ugh. I'm getting queasy already. The rolling and pitching of the amtrack in the unfriendly chop, combined with the deep vibration and nauseous fumes from the grumbling engine, have got me feeling like I don't know whether to shit or puke. Probably gonna do both. Claustrophobic confines of this floating farce don't help much either.

Christ! There goes Warner. Helmet off, head between knees, puking his guts out. A slimy pool of vomit flows rhythmically back and forth across the deck in unison with the 'track's motion. At the rear of the amtrack a couple of more Marines join Warner in a seasick symphony. Oh, god . . . I close my eyes and bury my face in my hands, trying to filter the sickening fumes, but it doesn't work and I'm heaving up the stew-on-rice from last night's chow which hasn't digested in a violent spray all over the deck and onto mine and poor Beard's boots. *Sorry about that shit, Beard.*

God, I'm sick. I went to sickbay, but the assholes said "fit for duty," even though I've had a fever and the shits for three days now. Just a mild bug, they said, nothing to worry about, but they don't hafta bounce and roll around in this puke-filled coffin. I'm so damn hot and dizzy and *oh christ, here it comes again. . . .*

Better now. Driver and crew have opened some hatches and the fresh salty breeze has chased the stinking fumes away. Cottony clouds and blue skies visible through a forward hatch near me. Feels good not to be shut up in the darkness.

I wonder if we're really going in this time, or is this just another dress rehearsal like yesterday? Damn, we flounced around in this iron tub for at least two hours thinking we were heading for the beach before finally going back to the ship. Just a "dry run." Dry my ass. Water splashed and sprayed into this bouncing bucket until I thought for sure we were going to join Davey Jones in his locker.

Brass said we needed the practice. Typical bullshit. Doesn't take a whole lot of skill to walk up a ramp, sit down and ride around for a couple of sickening, fun-filled hours, then walk down the ramp again. I guess the drivers needed practice to see just how much they could make these things rock and roll without actually capsizing and sinking. Our driver must've won, hands down.

Been at it for an hour now. Garcia just checked with the crew and passed the word that we're still circling in formation. No way to know yet if this is the real shit or not. The seas must've died down some because the ride is a whole lot smoother than it was yesterday or earlier today. My stomach's settled down, but my intestines feel all torn up and I need to crap real bad. If we don't hit the beach or go back to the ship soon I'm liable to spray it right in my pants. God, I'll be one popular bastard if that happens—you talk about *stink!* They'll probably throw my young ass overboard.

A sickly gurgling rumbles suddenly through my insides. I squeeze my rectum as tightly as I can in an effort to thwart the action of my protesting bowels. . . . *Whew!* Successful this time. I swear, if we go back to the ship I'm gonna go back to sickbay and shit all over their stainless steel table.

Late at night and I'm still awake. The soft glow from the lighted passageway creates fuzzy patterns on the shadowed overhead and deck. Low, monotonous humming from the distant engine room fails to lull me to sleep. Garbled snoring from one of the racks above my bottom berth aids my self-induced insomnia. Got a lot on my mind . . . a lot to think about.

Went back to sickbay after our second dry run in as many days and got bed rest again. Nice of the guys in the squad to insist I take the bottom rack. Less chance of them getting puked on or shit on if they're above me. Self-preservation. The couple of days' rest and some new medicine has done me a world of good. Stomach's settled down, and I don't feel like I'm gonna blow my asshole into orbit when I shit anymore. It was almost solid today. I'm still kinda weak, but I feel a hundred times better than I did before.

Our mail finally caught up with us today. I had a few letters and the hometown newspaper. Shocked to see on the front page that Richard Monigham was killed-in-action a couple of weeks ago. He was my recruiter's son. Went to high school with him. He quit school a few months before graduation and joined the Marines. There was a nice article and picture in the paper of his proud father swearing him in. Like father, like son; gonna make a career out of the Corps. Damn. Wonder how Gunny Monigham feels now? Like shit, I bet. Rough blow.

There's been a lot of scuttlebutt going around the ship the past few days about where we're headed. Some say the word is that the Marines are gonna push through the DMZ and invade the North, and that we're going to make a landing along the coast of North Vietnam as flank support. Others swear they heard from sources in "Officer Country" that we're headed for Korea to retake the USS *Pueblo* that the North Koreans captured last week. Another rumor is that the NVA are about to make a big push across the "Z" into the South.

I don't know what to believe about any of this crap. I hope it's all a bunch of bullshit and we stay on board ship for the rest of my tour. The ship's been heading north for the last day and a half though, so there must be something going on. And those landing rehearsals with the amtracks—something big must be up. I hope we're gonna invade the North. Go in there and kick their asses and get this shit over with. Frustrating as hell to make contact with the gooks only to have them di-di back across the DMZ where we can't touch 'em. What kinda fucked-up war is this, anyway? Those fuckers can come across and hit us on our side, but we can't cross over to theirs. Shit. That's like playing football and giving the ball back to the other team whenever we reach the fifty-yard line. Screw that. Maybe those idiots in Washington finally got their heads out of their asses and are gonna let us win this thing. Fucking-A! I hope we're going North.

It'll be some bad shit for sure, but it's better to die attacking them on their soil than to sit back and wait for them to hit us whenever and wherever they choose. That seems to be the general feeling throughout the company. If we're going back in the shit, let's take it to *them!*

Need to get some sleep. I turn from my back onto my right side, facing the darkness which coats the gray bulkhead. Damn. Still can't sleep. Been tossing and turning for hours. Tired . . . I know it's just wishful thinking that we won't get back into the shit sooner or later. But it's been so nice not being shot at and not being afraid these past couple of weeks that I can't help but wish . . . Oh well, like my daddy used to say, *"Wish in one hand and shit in the other, and see which one gets filled up first.*" Sound wisdom. No doubt I'll have *both* hands full of shit before that dream comes true.

I know we're going in sooner or later, but the thought scares me. Too many close calls already. Fresh out of rabbits feet and four-leaf clovers. Damn, how can anybody get through a whole tour of this shit alive and in one piece? I've seen 'em go out dead and in pieces. Dykes, Gabriel, and a few others. But hell, Porter just rotated back to the World, and so did Jackson from first platoon. They sure as hell saw their share of the shit, and they made it. Fuck it. I guess it's all in the cards.

Speaking of cards, I've got my helmet all decked out with a pair of "aces and eights." Dead man's hand. That's what ol' Wild Bill Hickok was holding in his poker hand when that fucker came up behind him and blew his shit away in Deadwood, South Dakota. Pair of aces and a pair of eights. Got 'em tucked under my rubber helmet band. I'm not really superstitious, but Porter told me before he left that it seems like the guys who get zapped never have shit on their helmet covers. He said the guys who make it are the ones that flaunt Death in its own face. I don't know if there's anything to all that shit or not, but he kept an ace of spades in the front and back of his helmet, and had a big target drawn on the back of his flak jacket. Rotated back home with just a scratched hand from a piece of shrapnel at Con Thien. On the other hand, Dykes got his shit totally blown away within three weeks. He didn't have anything on his helmet cover or flak jacket. Might be nothing to it, but I've had a target over the left breast of my flak jacket and the front of my helmet since my first month in-country. And I feel a whole lot better now, with my "aces and eights." You never know.

The sky is a threatening gray overcast, making it seem more like late afternoon than morning. Gone are the blue skies and playful cotton ball clouds of the past week. The change in weather befits the sullen mood that hangs over the company assembled in full combat gear on the open deck of the *Cleveland.* We're going in. Back aboard ship for just ten days, and we're going in. One pipe dream shot to hell.

Can you believe this shit? We practice making amphibious landings time after time and now we're going in by chopper! All that rocking and rolling and bouncing and puking for nothing. No storming the beaches like John Wayne this time. Kinda glad about it, though. The sea looks awfully rough today. It would be one hellacious ride in.

Oh god, here we go. The flight of Sea Knights from the *Iwo Jima* have landed, and we're being waved aboard. Sprinting for our bird with one hand holding my helmet from blowing off in the rotor wash and the other toting my M-16. Heavier than usual pack with rations, mortar and rocket rounds. Usual can of gun ammo slung over my left shoulder. They sure as hell have our asses weighted down this time. Wonder when we'll get back to the ship? Getting real used to the comforts of swabbie life.

Increased RPMs of straining engines. Vibration and din of racket growing. Lifting off, nose tilted, sharp banking to the right. Right leg straining to keep body upright. Squirming deeper into canvas webbed seat. Bottom dropping out of stomach as we rapidly gain altitude.

Word passes to get ready. Jesus. Much too short of a ride. Should've took longer. Fear and apprehension growing. Cold and clammy hands. Mouth is dry, suddenly thirsty. Dropping . . . dropping . . . dropping . . . touchdown. Ramp falls. Running down ramp into ugly gray day and tangled green LZ.

Back to the war.

18

Cold LZ. God, what a relief! I've been dreading this moment since before we left Subic Bay. Visions of bloody beachheads and shot-down choppers fading fast. Fear-wracking butterflies fleeing my gut, taking nausea with them. LZ and surrounding area secured. Saddled up and moving out.

The company is strung out in a long, slow-moving column. The trail winds through rolling hills of dense, low-growing bushes and trees. Misty tentacles reach down from the dreary sky and turn the foliage in the distance a depressing black. Cool, damp breeze blows steadily in our faces.

Word is we're in Thua Thien Province. Nobody seems to know exactly where, at least not us peons. Garcia said we'd be landing somewhere to the west of Hue, maybe near Camp Evans. That's way below the DMZ; the battalion's old AO before they moved north last summer. Not much happening here, from what I've heard. So secure they're bringing the Army up to take over the area. This op oughta be pretty much of a skate. I guess the brass just wanted to fuck with us a little bit, before we got too used to the ease and comfort of shipboard life.

Sporadic popping of rifles from up near the front of the column and we instinctively fan out and hit the deck facing outboard on either side of the trail. Shit's starting already. First platoon must've seen something. We wait uneasily, peering anxiously across the bleak landscape, resigning ourselves to the fact that the inevitable has finally arrived. Hearts pounding, temples throbbing, panting like dogs in heat. Waiting . . . firing slackens, ceases. Charlie must've hauled ass.

Distant *whump* of rotors coming from the heavy cloud cover, growing louder and louder. Someone has popped yellow smoke at the front of the column; it drifts toward us and dissipates into the gloom. Medevac. Damn, somebody's hit already. Chopper drops from the low ceiling and disappears beyond a small hill a couple of hundred meters ahead. Up again, invisible in the monsoon curtain, sound heading south. Probably bound for Phu Bai. Strange feeling of envy. Maybe a "million-dollar wound." Lucky fucker will probably be home in a couple of weeks. Could be KIA, though, or all fucked up. Might be preferable to this shit. Oh well, just ten more months to go. Up and humping.

At it again this morning. Aching muscles from another miserable night. Only goddamn kind of night there is in this fucking place—miserable. Still wet from the steady drizzle all night long, but the sun's out now and it won't take long for the red mud to dry out to red dust. A silver lining in every cloud, they say, but what the fuck do *they* know?

We've got the point for the column. Lucky us. Still following the well-used trail. I don't like this shit, but the terrain is so thick around here that it would take forever to cut our way through the bush. Banks is out front, keeping to the right side of the trail. I'm staggered behind him about ten meters away, followed by Warner and so on. The pace Banks sets would make a turtle proud. Just the way I like it. A couple of times already this morning word has been passed up from back in the column, wanting to know why our progress has been so slow:

"Oh, gee guys. Sorry about the holdup. It's just that me and ol' Banks here have this silly aversion to getting our shit blown away by these booby-traps we're finding all over this nice trail you've ordered us to diddy-bop down."

Banks looks back and motions for me to stop. Jesus, another one. He places a wad of C-ration shit paper in his mouth to moisten it, and drops it carefully beside a suspicious-looking area of disturbed earth near the center of the path. This booby-trap shit is making me nervous as hell. Fuckers are all over the place. Not like up north. Shit. Keeping my eyes on the ground almost constantly. Not paying enough attention to the bush around us. Gotta keep a better lookout for gooks to cover Bank's young ass, but I don't wanta blow my shit away on some damn mine or booby-trap either. Fucked Gabriel *all* up. Arm bones sticking out every which way, almost no meat left. Don't want no Bouncing Betty flying up my ass and blowing my balls off. Rather just get zapped nice and clean if I'm gonna get it. Fuck them assholes back there telling us to "step it up." They are most welcome to come up here and take the point and *sprint* down this trail if they want to. Fuck 'em.

We creep on, each man making sure the one following him sees the marked danger. Each man hoping the ones ahead don't fuck up and miss something. The farther you are back in the column, the less chance you have of tripping something. Pleasant thought—only Banks ahead of me. Poor him.

Mid-afternoon now. Left that awful, asshole-tightening trail a couple of hours ago and headed east across low undulating hills and shallow grassy valleys. Vegetation has thinned out considerably. Easy humping. Glad to be off that trail. Understatement. *Overjoyed* to be off that trail! Think I'd rather be up north tangling with the NVA than fucking around down here with all this booby-trap bullsh—

On the ground before the initial burst of AK-47 fire is over. Fairly close, but not aimed my way. Off the right flank, well back in the column. Action heating up now, popping and cracking exchanges spreading up and down the company. Still nothing real close to us. Can't see shit, as usual. Firing seems to be coming from the far side of a hill to our right front which the trail skirted. Middle of the column blasting away. Gooks have got their shit together—that's where the CP group is.

Lieutenant Simpson's talking excitedly on the horn with the Skipper. Word is passed for our platoon to get on-line and sweep the hill ahead of us. That'll flank their asses and give us the high ground. Shit. I hope they aren't trying to sucker us up that hill into a big-time ambush. Remembering the booby-trapped arty round on that other hill. Might not be so lucky this time. Why can't we just stay here?

Shit! Double-timing, scrambling up the hill, cold sweat or is it raining again? Icy nausea gripping my gut again. Never get used to this shit . . . just waiting for it to happen . . . come on goddammit gooks don't make us wait get it the fuck over with not so bad after it starts it's the waiting that gets you come on come on almost there almost there. . . .

We gain the top of the hill, uncontested. Spreading out, taking up prone or kneeling firing positions overlooking sharp dropoff and the valley beyond. Smoke and muzzle flashes visible from a little ridge rising from the valley floor like a thick scab on a hairy arm. Still over two hundred meters out—a lot farther than I thought.

Our gun teams have set up and their red tracers glow brilliantly against the gloom as they join others from first and third platoons in beautiful crisscross patterns of destruction. *Get some, guns!*

Whumping rotors beat across the threatening sky. A Huey gunship materializes overhead from nowhere, like a pissed-off hornet determined to sting the shit out of somebody. Angled dive, guns chattering. Sudden puffs of smoke like a silent backfire as several rockets swoosh from their pods, streaking with orange fury and exploding in angry red and black clouds upon the ridge. Watching in fascination as the gunship banks in a tight circle and unleashes another load of flashing destruction toward the scabby ridge. Flaming mushrooming clouds followed by sharp cacophony of explosions. Pinpoint accuracy. Out-fucking-standing!

Booming report of outgoing artillery from a nearby battery sounds peaceful and reassuring. Spending the night at Camp Evans, Two-Four's former base camp. Snug as a bug in a fucking rug. Sandbagged wall tent, wooden deck, cot—the works. No hole-watch or LPs or ambushes. Another skate.

Humped into Evans just before dark. The Army's 101st Airborne Division is taking over here. These fuckers have got everything. More choppers than you can shake a stick at. All Hueys. None of the antiquated '34s the Crotch uses. Saw a few Cobra gunships. Mean looking motherfuckers. Shark-toothed painted "faces." Sleek narrow fuselage with piggyback cockpit. Armed to the hilt. Christ, those bastards must be something in action. Never saw one before. Hope we get 'em, but I doubt it. Shit, we're still humping WWII-vintage packs, while the doggies use the modern rucksacks that support the weight of the load a lot easier. Fucking NVAs got better shit than we do. Aw, quit bitching. Small price to pay for being a member of the greatest fighting force the world has ever known. Right.

Found out at chow tonight who the WIA from yesterday was. It was Lance Corporal Darden, from first platoon. I went through ITR and staging with him. Never liked him at all. A bully and a braggart who thought his shit didn't stink. Gonna show all of us what a *real* Marine was when we got to Nam. He showed us, all right. Chickenshit asshole shot himself in the foot. Self-inflicted. No accidental discharge, either. When the shit broke out yesterday, his squad leader saw him do it. Son of a bitch probably thought he was gonna skate back to the World with a million-dollar wound and a purple heart. Instead, he'll get busted to private and probably do hard-time at Portsmouth, followed by a dishonorable discharge. Gutless shit should've shot himself through the fucking head.

God, will this shit never cease? Last night I was warm, dry, safe and comfortable in a rack at Camp Evans. Tonight I'm wet, cold, depressed and scared shitless in a muddy hole somewhere near Con Thien, less than a klick below the DMZ. Gale-force wind blowing sheets of rain almost horizontally with stinging effect. Shivering uncontrollably from the teeth-chattering chill. Mournful howling wind from the throat of the pitch-black night heaps more fuel on the fire of my discontent. Near total misery. Misery loves company. Well, the motherfucker's got a whole company of grunts out here in this mess to love tonight. Doing a damn fine job of it, too. Shit.

Choppered up here early this morning. Set-in as a blocking force to intercept a large NVA element that's supposed to be moving across the "Z" for a big push. Word is that the shit is hitting the fan all over the place. Khe Sanh to the west is under attack. Quang Tri City's getting hit hard. Hue City's in gook hands already. Shit, we were right near there yesterday. Wonder why they sent us up here. Seems like they would've sent us to Hue since we were already practically there. Fucking brass is amazing.

The shit is bad all over, most affirmed, but we had no

contact at all today. Either S-2 fucked up, or the NVA are playing hide-and-seek. Supposed to move out early tomorrow and find Mr. Charles, wherever he may be. Bad shit brewing. Chances of getting back to the ship anytime soon looking very slim. Fuck it. Nice while it lasted.

The Sea Knight swoops low over the beautiful green jungled hills and sets down on the bare red earth of the LZ. Ramp drops. Out we go, eyes squinting against the sandblasting rotor wash. Welcome to Camp Carroll. Small plateau surrounded on three sides by high mountain ridges. Word is there's supposed to be a division of gooks out there somewhere, intent on taking out the big 175mm batteries here that are firing support for the Marines at Khe Sanh. Monsoons have seriously hampered air support for the besieged grunts there. If the NVA take these big guns, they will be in a true world of hurt.

They've got our battalion spread out way too thin along Highway 9, much of which Mr. Charles controls now. Things aren't looking too awfully bright at the moment.

We saddle-up and pass through the relative safety of Camp Carroll's perimeter and head down the road into the foreboding valley below. Wonderful. One company of Marines to fight off a reported division of NVA. Feeling naked and vulnerable . . . I should've joined the fucking Air Force or gone to college or Canada or something. Way to go, Mikey.

19

In the valley and digging-in atop a grassy knoll as fast as the protesting rocky ground will allow. Entrenching tools and clawing fingers send showers of red earth and rocks out of our deepening holes to the accompaniment of frantic curses and sharp *karrumph* of exploding mortar rounds falling upon Camp Carroll.

Groundhog time. Camp Carroll's taking incoming and it's just a matter of time before the gooks in the surrounding mountains notice what we're up to and start pounding our young asses. "Dig 'em deep," Lieutenant Simpson said. Fucking-A to that, Sir. The echoing hollow *thoomp* of mortar rounds leaving their tubes is all the incentive needed for us to get down to some serious excavating.

Beard lets loose a flurry of oaths in that strange Maine accent as his E-tool strikes another big rock with a dull clang. I stumble across the irregular bottom of our narrow, nearly six-foot-long foxhole, and together we wrestle the boulder from the earth and heave it like a huge shot put over the lip of our chest-deep haven. Damn rock must weigh two hundred pounds at least. We flop down on our asses and lean our sweat-soaked backs against the cool damp wall, exhausted. I look over at Beard. Beads of red-dish-brown sweat gather and flow in little rivulets down his face and neck, diverted only by bushy eyebrows and the sparse beginnings of a mustache he's determined to grow. Simultaneously, our faces break and we grin that grin at each other that says, "Yeah, I'm scared and I can see you are too but there ain't a whole hell of a lot we can do about it now so what the fuck?" and then we're back on our feet and digging.

It's Larson's turn to dig again. He jumps into the hole as I scramble out, grab my rifle, bandoliers, flak jacket and helmet, and scurry in a low crouch to a small gully pro-tected by some boulders and low bushes about fifty feet below our hole. I squirm my way as close as possible between the rocks and peer through the sparse bush to the jungle a hundred meters downhill. Good field of fire that way. I lift my head and my eyes follow the high ridges that encompass our valley on three sides. Jesus. I suddenly feel like I felt that time at the beach when the rough surf pounded me under and pulled my swimsuit down around my ankles. Naked. A thousand eyes are watching me, see-ing me in my humiliation and embarrassment, as sights align and fingers tighten for the squeeze that will splatter my brains against this rock and send my carcass home in a box, and suddenly I want very much to be back up the slope in that unfinished hole with Beard and Larson beside me and . . . come on, stop this shit! Get a grip on yourself, asshole. Can't afford to lose it now. Gotta get my shit together. Okay, so there's thousands of gooks up in those

ridges, and it's a sure bet they've got sniper teams up there
somewhere, but you've got a good position here. They
probably can't even see you from this angle, so quit worrying about something that's not going to happen. And anyway, if it does you'll never know what hit you, so fuck it.

I lean a little closer to the rocks and listen to the
incoming still pounding Camp Carroll back up on the
plateau. Poor bastards. Better them than us. Not so heavy
now, anyway. Glancing back at the grassy knoll, I see our
company's position resembles a prairie dog town. Heads
and shoulders popping above ground, then suddenly disappearing again. Flurries of red earth leaping skyward,
then falling and scattering to form powdery parapets
around each fighting hole. Here and there an earthen-col-
ored grunt scampers from one hole to another to relay a
message or take his turn at digging. Working feverishly,
like squirrels gathering nuts to beat the deadline of the
approaching harsh winter. Except the only nuts we're trying to save here are our own, and the winter's blast from
which we seek shelter will be a blizzard of hot steel from
mortars, rockets and recoilless rifles. Spring suddenly
seems a long way off.

Warner is back, and his shit is shook. That pimply-
faced Texan has been having hell with his acne for weeks,
so after just a couple of days here Doc Poteat sent him on
a chopper to Delta Med at Dong Ha for treatment. Lucky
bastard spent two days lying in a real rack between clean
sheets with moist compresses on his face. Hot chow. Even
had a genuine round-eyed officer-type nurse or two on
the ward. Blue-balls City. They gave him some pills and

several tubes of ointment and sent him back to the bush.

While he was waiting for his chopper, a medevac landed with a bunch of wounded on board. Warner was helping the docs unload the wounded, and was carrying a stretcher case when the wind or rotor wash blew the poncho off the guy they were humping. Warner was carrying the rear of the stretcher and got himself a bird's-eye view. Both of the poor dude's legs were blown off at the hips, and his dick and balls were gone, just like somebody had taken an ice cream scooper and cleanly scooped them away. Just some indented red meat where the jewels should've been, hardly any blood. Looked like a department store mannequin with no legs, he said. Except the guy kept screaming about his legs being gone, and kept asking a corpsman who flew in from the bush with him about his family jewels, and the doc kept lying to the poor fucker, saying he was going to be okay and that everything was fine and not to worry, and poor ol' Warner just couldn't hack it and commenced to puke up all that good hot chow from his last meal all over his chest and the lower part of the stretcher he was carrying, but it didn't get on the wounded dude with no legs or dick or balls because he was just half there anyway. . . .

Aw, shit! The small bush I had grabbed to help pull myself up the steep slope just uprooted, and I go sliding down the embankment on my belly over loose rocks and mud as slick as goose shit for at least fifteen feet. That's about the tenth time today that's happened. I scrape and shake mud, rocks and leaves out of my utilities and once again curse the day I ever read those bullshitting recruiting posters at the post office with those Hollywood Marines in their spiffy dress blues.

Hoppy snickers behind me. "Keep your proper interval, Marine," he says, a shit-eating grin spread across his muddy pale-moon face. I tell Mr. Cowboy-fucking-Kid to shove a saddle horn up his bowlegged ass, then turn and start pulling myself up the face of Mount Everest again.

Near the crest, Larson holds onto a small tree with one hand and extends his rifle, butt-first, toward me with the other. My mud-caked fingers find the grip of the M-14, and with Larson's tug-o'-war pull and my ten-pounds-apiece boots digging desperately for footholds, I finally manage to scale the top. I take my turn at the tree, offering my '16 to Hoppy and fighting off the temptation to let go and watch him tumble down the hill like a muddy snowball, a look of surprised bewilderment on his dirty little-boy face. Nah, I can't do that. Hoppy's a good dude. With a straining grunt I yank him up and over, leaving Hoppy to help the next guy while I fan out to help provide security while the rest of the squad makes it up the slope.

Been on patrol since daylight, leaving our lines and heading into the foothills to the west that rise to form one side of the horseshoe-shaped ridge line surrounding our valley. It's been uphill and uphill and more uphill all goddamn morning. Feel like a damn mountain goat, except mountain goats traverse their range on their feet, not by slipping and sliding around on their asses and bellies like a mud snake. I'm not the Lone Ranger; everybody's been busting their ass on this hump. Hell, Ortea dropped his M-60 when he slipped and the damn gun slid fifty feet if it went an inch. Had to stop and clean it. Even changed the barrel, there was so much mud packed in it.

Damn sure glad we got a gun team with us. Ortea is one gutsy bastard. Needs a wheelbarrow to carry his balls in. With the way the gooks have been hitting our patrols, it's comforting to know that if we hit the shit and holler "guns up!" Ortea and Willis will be there.

Up on the point with Banks now. I hack at the choking jungle with a machete while Banks strains to see through the all-but-impenetrable foliage, his '16 ready on full automatic. Soaked through to the skin from a combination of sweat and constant rain. At least I think it's still raining. Hard to tell in this triple canopy. Water could drip off these leaves forever after a good downpour, I guess.

Been at this shit for hours, it seems. My right arm feels like it's gonna fall off, and my blisters have got blisters on top of them. *Christ!* Something scurries away through the wet leaves under my feet. My already pounding heart pounds harder. A rat or snake or something . . . I don't need this shit. We'd be in a real world of hurt if we needed a medevac in this fucked-up place. You get hit here and you might as well go ahead and kiss your ass goodbye. No way a chopper could get in, and the thought of carrying somebody back down this fucking mountain . . . forget it. You get hit bad up here, you better hope you die outright.

Finally cut our way out of the thick shit and found an old trail that seems to follow the top of the ridge line. The bush is not too thick on either side, so we're staying the fuck off of it. Moving cautiously, parallel with the trail, for as long as we can, forty or fifty meters away.

Me and Banks see 'em at the same time and drop down

together like a synchronized swim team. *Gooks! Boo-coo gooks!* A whole shitpot full of gooks, moving down the trail, armed with AKs, light machine guns, RPGs, mortars and supplies and Jesus there must be a hundred of 'em!

We look back to signal the rest of the squad, but they've all seen what's happening and are spread out, hiding and hugging Mother Earth for all they're worth. Please, please, don't anybody cough or sneeze or scratch or fart and I sure hope everybody ate their Cs this morning because this horde of gooks are being awfully quiet and we wouldn't want any hungry stomachs growling at this most inopportune time and giving us away now, would we?

We wait at least half an eternity after the NVA are out of sight before we dare to move a muscle. Poor ol' Gray, who is so short he's down to three weeks and a wake up, and got stuck with being squad leader because Garcia *would* choose now to go on his fucking R&R, wonders whether we should call in the movement or not. We all confer and elect unanimously to let "mum be the word." Fucking brass would probably make us camp out along this gook highway forever if they knew what we just saw. So, nobody saw shit, right guys? Fucking-A to that.

Continuing on, at a hurried pace now. The trail led us out of the jungle and onto a beautiful open grassy area atop the high ridges. Rocky outcroppings jut upward on either side of the golden grassy meadow we've been humping through for the last half hour. Gray stops and studies his map, and takes another compass reading. He decides to angle off to our right, down a series of hills which should lead us to a point just below our lines, he thinks. Wants to know what we think. Sounds good to us, ol' Fearless Leader. Of course, if you've fucked up reading the map we could wind up somewhere in Laos or North Vietnam, but hey, don't let that thought bother you. Goes with the territory. All a part of being a "leader of men." So lead on, Corporal Gray, we're right behind you.

The grassy slope runs out several hundred meters from the bottom of the hill, and we're forced to worm our way through jungle growth again. It's late in the afternoon and we're just about beat. Gray's conscience has got the better of him, and he's up near the point with Larson. Not a real smart thing to do, considering he's carrying Garcia's M-79. If the point gets taken out he might go too, and we'd need the firepower the blooper offers too much for him to be up there. At least the jungle's not too thick here. Able to go over, under or around most of this tangled shit instead of having to hack our way thr—

Choommb—thwack! Jesus H. Christ! What the fuck?

Sudden loud crack above my head, just behind me. I watch in horrid fascination as the crumpled, gold-colored high explosive M-79 round falls and spins crazily like a child's toy top on the jungle floor at my feet. Around and around and around in terrifyingly tight circles, gradually giving way to wider and more erratic revolutions, until it finally dances off with a quick dash to rest silently and innocently upon the vegetated carpet.

I continue to stare, fascinated, not really comprehending what's happened until Gray comes running back down the squad, all hollowed-eyed and terror-stricken and "Oh my god I'm sorry" written all over his face. The grenade launcher got tangled up in the thick brush and somehow the safety got pushed off and the trigger tripped and a round fired but it didn't go quite far enough to arm and explode and it hit right above my fucking head and dropped practically at my feet and spun and spun but didn't go *boom* and don't worry about it Gray it could've happened to anybody you're just not used to the blooper it's not your fault really no sweat never mind that an air-burst would've taken mine and Hoppy's and Beard's and who knows who else's heads off hey don't worry about it it's no big deal. . . .

How about that shit! Ol' Gray had it figured out almost letter perfect. We're in the jungle edge just below our lines, maybe a hundred meters away. Already radioed in to alert the lines that we're coming in. Gonna pop a green cluster just in case for extra precaution. Green fireballs arcing through the dark, cloudy sky like a Roman candle. Moving toward the lines with excessive noise and verbal communication with the grunts in the holes. What a hump this one's been. One more day off my calendar . . . ten more years off my life.

Today is Sunday. I know that because this morning as me and Banks were enjoying a cup of that horrible swill he calls coffee, a crowd began gathering up the knoll near the company CP. Word came down that the battalion chaplain was gonna hold an interdenominational service for all faiths, and that everyone not on watch was encouraged to attend. Seems the brass detected our morale has been sagging a bit as of late, so they figured a good dose of ecclesiastical bullshit from the senior sky pilot might be just the remedy to put things back in their proper perspectives.

Not yet being confirmed atheists, me and ol' Banks

sauntered up the hill, more to break up our routine of boredom than to hear the message of "God loves you and the Red, White and Blue." Talked on and on about how it was "God's will" that we're here as "fine Christian soldiers engaged in the noble cause of stemming the tide of the godless communists seeking to destroy the God-given rights of the brave South Vietnamese people who are the children of God" just as much as our own mothers and fathers and brothers and sisters back home in the good ol' U.S. of A.

Started spouting about how the Lord was always beside us to guide and protect us when suddenly that distinctive hollow *thoommp* began echoing through "the valley of the shadow of death," and us grunts began hauling ass to the nearest available hole. Left the poor ol' sky pilot and his stunned enlisted assistant with Bibles in their hands and bewilderment on their faces. Wonder if the Lord followed them to their hole? He must have, because me and Banks looked and looked, and He sure as hell wasn't in ours.

First platoon hit the shit today while patrolling the valley below the eastern sector of our lines. Our platoon was the designated reactionary force, and we grabbed our gear and hauled ass at double-time toward their position in a matter of seconds after the initial call to the CP requesting assistance.

We ran past where the grassy slopes end, into an area dominated by thick, low-growing trees. A short way into this dwarf forest, the gooks opened up on us from the left flank. Our squad hit the deck, fanned out and returned fire while the other two squads continued on through the hail of bullets to the aid of first platoon. After a short while the firing ceased. We assessed our casualties. Only one WIA from our platoon. PFC Fielder, a black dude who's one of the newest guys in the outfit, took a round through and through the left cheek of his ass. Clean wound. Won't be gone more than a week, Doc Hamm says.

Fielder was grinning ear to ear, like a kid in a watermelon patch. Not sure whether it was from the thought of clean sheets and the "glory" of earning a purple heart, or the morphine Doc had just jammed in his hip. I'll put my money on the latter.

20

Listening post tonight, and guess who got tagged to be the lucky leader for this all-night gut-churner? Lucky me. Taking Beard and Warner with me. Won't hafta worry about them falling asleep on me. They're every bit as scared as I am. The NVA are crawling all over this valley, especially at night. Nearly every patrol the company's sent out lately has either made contact or reported movement. Outside the wire is not a nice place to be.

We move out at dusk, Warner on the point, me in the middle with the radio, and Beard behind me watching our rear real good. We head east a short ways down into the valley below our lines, and then turn south and follow a path that roughly parallels the road leading up the plateau toward Camp Carroll.

Our progress is painfully slow as we imagine a gook behind every bush that sways drunkenly in the brisk breeze and chilling shadows of the waning February day. But that's okay, because we're in no hurry to die anyway. Toward the west a large hawk-like bird flies on rapid wing beats as though desperately trying to catch the sun's last futile effort that glows reddish-orange above the crest of the black mountain ridges. A half mile away on the plateau, a battery of monstrous 175s fires at some distant unseen target, filling the valley with terrible pealing thunder like Mother Nature gone berserk.

About two hundred meters up the plateau I signal for Warner to stop, and we hide in a clump of bushes to await the cover of full darkness before crossing the road and setting-in for the night. SOP for LPs—stop in a "dummy" location just before dark in case the gooks have spotted you, then after it's good and dark and you can't see shit, you get up and feel your way a couple of hundred meters or so to another location.

We wait until the final shadows have been swallowed up by the cave-like blackness of the starless night before scampering across the road and groping our way another hundred and fifty meters or so into the scrub growth between our company's position and Camp Carroll above us. No safety intervals now. Almost asshole to bellybutton. Sure as shit don't want to get separated in this inkwell. Blind Man's Bluff was never like this. Feel, step, feel, step, a hundred times over. Hands fondling backs, gentle touches seeking security and comfort in a netherworld of insecurity and discomfort. Clutching for something that no longer exists in our harsh world, but that doesn't matter; there's at least a semblance of solace in the act itself.

I somehow find what seems to be a ring of bushes in the darkness, and we set-in. As good a place as we could hope for under the circumstances. Good concealment all around us. I key the handset and whisper that "Lima Papa Tango Tango is set-in." Warner helps me slide the radio off, and the cool night air kisses my sweaty back, sending an icy shiver up my spine. We place the radio between us in the center of our mini-perimeter, making sure the squelch button is fully on. This is not the ideal place to have static and unnecessary transmissions filling the air. Volume as low as possible.

I check the time, squinting at the luminous dial. 2040, I think. We'll wait another four or so, then take turns at two-hour watches. No sweat. Just sit real quiet, keep your ears open, and key the handset twice when the CP calls for a sit-rep. Nothing to it. Like a walk in the park. Yeah, right.

Our darting eyes and pained expressions tell each other that we really *did* hear what we thought we heard. Movement. Jesus. Shit. Easily discernible sounds of bushes scraping against clothing, and slight metallic rattling of equipment. I even think I hear mumbled voices, or is that just the wind? Hard to tell because the blood is racing through my veins and the pulsating of my throbbing temples sounds like a bass drum pounding in my head.

Up on our knees, straining the night with what little vision we've acquired toward the sounds. *Oh, god!*—figures looming like giants among a cluster of bushes, maybe fifty feet away! How many? Three? Four? A hundred? A thousand? I'm suddenly sick again, with cold dread. They aren't going away, they're just disappearing, dropping out of sight. Oh, Jesus, they're stopping and dropping just fifteen or twenty meters away! Setting-in for the night, or just a short pause to coordinate? How many? What am I

gonna do? Oh fuck—I'm in charge! My responsibility . . .
Who are they? Sappers? Ambush? A squad or a platoon or a
whole goddamn company or regiment of gooks getting
ready to hit our lines or Camp Carroll? How do I get into
these situations? Can't have just a normal, nothing-hap-
pens LP. No, gotta fucking *see* something again and they
can't just walk on by and leave us alone oh no they've gotta
fucking stop almost right in our laps. *Shit!*

Okay, okay . . . think now, *think*. You don't know who
they are or how many there are but you know they're
there and they haven't seen you so you've got the advantage on them for now if you don't fuck up. Call in the
movement but be *damn quiet* about it. . . . I grab the
handset and bury my face in my other arm pressed to
the ground and tell the CP that we've got movement but
the movement has quit moving and has decided to stop
just a few feet away from us and what should we do,
over?

The CP tells us to stay put *(no shit!),* remain calm
(sure) and alert *(of course, thanks for reminding us),* and
to report any further developments. Reassuring words of
wisdom from above. Now you bastards at the CP go on
back to sleep sorry to disturb you and don't worry about us
poor peons out here in the boonies we'll be fine and we
certainly won't be bored after all we'll have our whole lives
flashing before our eyes to keep us entertained all
night. . . . Shit.

I carefully remove the four fragmentation grenades from
my deep trouser pockets and straighten the pins. Arrange
several magazines of ammo within easy reach and feel. Beard
and Warner sense what I'm doing and follow suit.

It's decision time. I don't know how many there are, but if it's just a few I think we can take 'em out with a flurry of grenades and automatic fire before they know what hit 'em. But, if there's a lot of 'em, they'll probably react quick and zap our asses for sure. I only saw a few, I think. Bushes and shadows can sure play tricks on your eyes and senses . . . How many? . . . How many? . . . Wish I had a claymore set up. I'd blow their shit away for sure, then. But this is a fucking LP, not an ambush. Not out here to make contact, just observe and report. Okay. Attention, CP—I've observed two or three or a thousand unfriendlies out here and am reporting same. One slight problem. Said unfriendlies have apparently decided to stop right beside us for the night. Any suggestions? Shit.

My hand tightens its grip around the egg-shaped frag and my finger teases the looped pin a little farther out of the small hole in the spoon. To kill or not to kill, that is the question. To die or not to die . . . Do it! No, wait, don't. It's now or never! Wait and see. Blow 'em away now, before they discover you! Sit tight, they'll probably move on soon. They'll never know what hit 'em if you do it now! You might miss, or maybe there's too many. Hurry up before you miss your chance! Beard and Warner are *your* responsibility. . . .

Oh, Jesus, why me? My head aches and I'm sick and I'm in a cold sweat and I've got the power of life or death in my hands and on my shoulders make the decision to throw it and somebody's gonna die for sure them or us or maybe all of us or wait and see and maybe more of them are coming won't have a snowball's chance in Hell then but they might just go away and nobody'll get hurt I shouldn't have this shit on me nobody should but you've got to make a decision do something do something do something. . . .

A few minutes of forever pass, and I decide to sit tight and wait it out. I think we could probably take 'em out, but if we fuck up we might all buy the farm. Besides, even if we were lucky enough to zap 'em all, every gook in this whole fucking valley would be alerted, and there's no way in hell we'd make it back to our lines without getting our shit blown away. Yeah, good decision . . . we'll just sit still, be real quiet, and wait for them to leave. Good cover here. Probably couldn't see us even in the daylight. Just sit still and be ready and don't fuck up. Gonna be a long night, though. God, it's gonna be a long night.

Sitting and staring into the darkness like a zombie. Eyes too tired now to be sleepy. How long has it been? Hours, for sure. Seems like years. Every night sound wrenching our guts like medieval instruments of torture. Maybe this is forever. Hell has opened up and swallowed us and this is it. Eternal LP. With movement.

Time passing yet standing still, no longer existing. Wake up and die or just sit here and die, it doesn't matter anymore, does it? Maybe we're dead already and just don't know it. What is life, anyway? Supposed to be enjoyable, but I can't remember enjoyable anymore. Only tired, tired, and more tired. And fear. Yeah, full of fear, but if I'm dead what's to fear? So, just sit still and be quiet and nothing to fear but fear itself just tired . . . so tired.

Stay awake. Gotta stay awake. Shh . . . don't breathe so loud hey you two bastards awake? Eyes are open but even dead people have their eyes open can a person sleep with eyes open? Zombies can but they're really dead we've gotta stay awake so we don't die be real quiet no noise no noise their eyes are open so they must be okay they're so tired I know they're tired because I'm tired but we can sleep later if we stay awake stay alert no sleep no sleep gotta stay awake stay alert stay alive.

Roseola creeps up and over the dull charcoal ridges to the east and paints their crests with a faint pastel wash. Awakening jungle noises, like those from the Tarzan movies I watched as a kid, begin to sound from the tangled foothills above us as another day struggles to dawn. Unseen rays dilute the utter darkness and turn the sky a permeable gray. Hollowed eyes and burned brains snap to attention as the noisy commotion twenty meters away blows the fogginess from our minds and brings us to razor-sharp alertness.

One-two-three, the figures arise from the cover of the scrubby brush and begin to move out. Even in the piss-poor light there's no mistaking what we see. Marines. Fucking Marines! M-16s, PRC-25, sour expressions of lost sleep, mumbled grumblings of let-down guards. We sit quiet and watch in shocked disbelief until they have disappeared, angling uphill and toward the road that leads to Camp Carroll.

Jesus H. Christ! I am *pissed!* I am truly most affirmed pissed! Somebody back at the CP is fixing to catch hell from one lowly PFC. I came *that-fucking-close* to blowing those bastards away, and if I had they would've died and maybe we *all* would've died and who the hell put two LPs in the same area? Worthless sons-of-bitching brass-fucking office pogue rear-echelon bastards can't even get their shit together enough to keep LPs away from each other so we don't blow our own shit away! Goddamn 'em, *and* their fucked-up war!

From here on out, I'm in this shit strictly to save my own young ass, and my buddies'. Screw the whole worthless rest of 'em.

21

Moved our position this morning across the road to the eastern slope of our knoll. The vegetation's a lot thicker on this side, so we took turns at digging our new fighting holes and cutting fields of fire in the brush. Then we strung rolls and rolls of concertina wire about thirty meters in front of our position, and rigged trip flares and C-ration cans with small rocks in 'em among the wire. Makes a nice burglar alarm for probing NVA.

Got into a heated but friendly argument with some splibs from first squad (who think they're the Temptations) over music. We were stringing wire and Morton was singing some Hank Williams favorites in that unforgiving voice of his, and the splibs—Turnage, Fielder and Huggins—were nearby, torturing our ears with their pitiful imitation of Motown falsetto. Our working parties got closer and closer, and before long the air was rent with a god awful combination of country-western/Motown-jive that was enough to gag a maggot and knock a buzzard off a gut wagon.

Turnage hollered at Morton to "Knock off that white trash honky cowboy moaning and groaning shit," and Morton fired back that their "singing" sounded like "a pack of fucking dogs howling at the moon," and to "shove it up your fat black ass."

Being the modest mediator that I am, I told 'em all to shut the fuck up, and that the Beatles made country music *and* soul music sound like a bunch of shit anyway. Then I started singing "Yesterday" to prove my point, and the splibs started ranting and raving about how the Beatles stole that song from Ray Charles. Jesus H. Christ, I couldn't believe it. Must've spent fifteen minutes arguing over who wrote it. Never could convince 'em it was Lennon and McCartney. Finally just let it drop and we continued on, stringing wire, sounds of Detroit going one way and Nashville heading the other.

Spent the rest of the afternoon digging a sleeping hooch into the steep slope which rises directly behind our squad's fighting holes. Dug a ways into the hill, and then extended our "cave" with walls of several layers of sandbags. Stretched a couple of ponchos over the top for a roof. That'll keep out the rain and sun, if it ever shines again, but won't be worth a shit when we take incoming. We plan to make a real roof if we can get some timbers, but for now it's the best we can do. Beats sleeping in the rain.

Pulling hole watch with Morton. Too early for either one of us to try to sleep, so we sit on the back edge with our legs dangling in the hole. Been a long day. Feeling tired, sort of melancholy.

"What day is this, Chuck?" I ask, opening my supper of

ham and mothers, feeling my way around the lip of the
can in the darkness with my C-rat opener.

"Friday, I think. Maybe Saturday," he answers in that
bland, not-quite-country and not-quite-big-city Midwestern drawl.

I opt for Friday. "Friday night," I muse. "You know what
I'd be doing tonight if I was home?"

He looks at me with that "I don't really give a shit what
you'd be doing, but I know you're gonna tell me, so go
ahead" look as I continue.

"Well, this being February, football season would be
over so I wouldn't be at the game. I'd be over at the Youth
Center down the street from the stadium, and I'd be on
stage with my band playing the latest hits and watching all
them tits and asses bumping and jiggling. And afterwards,
when the dance was over, I'd pick me up one of them girls
that's always making goo-goo eyes at the band, and we'd
go cruising downtown around the city marina, then
around Jimmy's Drive-In to get a hamburger and some
french fries and a Coke. Then we'd probably drive over
through the Cove, and my friend Tom would turn on the
headlights of his '57 Chevy as we ride along them winding
roads to scare the shit out of the girls, and they'd scream
and laugh and rub all over us, for "protection," you know.
Then we'd probably ask the girls if they wanted to go drive
out to the beach and watch the submarine races for a
while."

I glance out of the corner of my eye at Morton, who
looks a little more interested, but confused. "Submarine
races? They have submarine races in Florida?"

Jesus, what a dumb ass. "Sure, Chuck," I lie, struggling

to keep a straight face. "You mean to tell me y'all big-city dudes from Chicago ain't never been to a submarine race? Shit. You're joking, huh?"

He looks at me, all serious-like, and shakes his head. "No, I never heard of it."

"Oh, come on, Chuck, quit shitting me. I thought y'all damn Yankees taught us poor ol' backward dumbass rebels everything we know. Y'all must have 'em up there in big ol' Lake Michigan." Baiting him now . . . waiting for the big bite.

"No, really, never heard of it," he says, looking rather pensive now, rubbing the stubble of unshaved fuzz on his grubby face. "How do they tell who wins?"

I can't stand it any longer. I roll on my side, fighting back the laughter, choking on stifled guffaws, tears streaming down my cheeks. I *got* him—hook, line and sinker! Oh, my aching sides.

Startled awake by the dreaded and unmistakable sound of exploding gunfire. Momentarily confused, trying to get my bearings in the dark. Oh yeah, inside the new hooch. Morton's got the last watch, so I came back here to sleep. Feeling around, find my helmet and slap it on. Grab my rifle and bandoleers from the corner, push the poncho hatch cover aside and stumble out into the chilly damp night. Somebody bumps into my back, almost knocking me down.

"Larson?"

"Yeah!"

"Jesus H. Christ. Let's get to the fucking hole."

We half-run and half-feel our way to the fighting hole

on the left side of our squad's area of responsibility, and drop in beside Morton who's working the darkness over for signs of movement with fervent eyes.

"Anything?" Larson asks, resting his M-14 on the sand-bag parapet.

"Don't see shit except for those muzzle flashes down there," he answers, pointing into the void of the valley below. Dozens of orange-white flashes like a myriad of flashbulbs going off dot the inky landscape.

Above our heads that awful angry sound of air-sucking buzzes and snaps fills the night like a hive of pissed-off nocturnal hornets. The hill behind us resounds with heavy *thumps* and high-pitched *bazziinnngs* as hundreds of rounds slam into the ground or ricochet off rocks, streaking into the black sky like a fusillade of bottle rockets. An occasional sharp *boom* of exploding grenades sounds from various points up and down our lines as scared Marines with adrenaline rushes strike out at shadows and bushes which might be, or harbor, gooks. The more distant staccato chattering of machine guns opens up from several points, and showers of green and red tracers fly at us like someone kicking the dying embers of a campfire. The terrible *screech-boom* of incoming rockets adds yet another fearful aspect to the growing nightmare. Most of them seem to pass well over our position and slam farther up the hillside.

Still no real targets and almost no return fire from our side. Good fire discipline. Don't give away our positions with muzzle flashes until we have to. High on the knoll near the road the rumbling roar of diesel engines sounds through the noise of battle as the tanks which have been spread along the road between us and Camp Carroll maneuver into position to fire their 90mm cannon into the valley.

Baboom! Terrific tongue of red-orange flame spits a deadly shell through the darkness to explode like a crashing thunderbolt barely a hundred meters in front of our hole. Jesus H. Christ—hey, that was awfully close, guys! Hope those tank jockeys know what the hell they're doing . . . *oh shit!*

There's no time to worry about the tanker's aim now, because we're hearing the terribly loud noise of rattling cans in the wire just below us and pop flares go off and shadows flow from the bushes and take shape with heads and arms and legs and we suddenly have targets many many targets boo-coo fucking targets and god it's just like being back at Geiger on the John Wayne course with all those pop-up targets where we shot 'em dead from the hip but these targets don't seem to fall so easily and they're shooting back and there's screaming and hollering and things blowing up all over and the noise is awful keep firing and throwing grenades over there in the wire god the tracers the tracers must be a million of 'em only every fifth round but must be millions over there over there slap another magazine in not jammed just empty pull the pin and let it fly always had a good arm can't let 'em get close cut 'em down throw over there in the wire keep firing reload reload got plenty but don't waste it fire discipline but keep firing keep firing keep firing. . . .

Gray dawn. Misty and wet. Dirty-cotton sky. Faint filtered glow above the mountain ridge beyond the valley.

Nothing ever looked so beautiful. I look around. Larson and Morton are beautiful with their mud-splattered tattered utilities and bloodshot eyes. This miserable fucking hole with its carpet of spent brass casings is beautiful. All those dead fucking gooks tangled up in the wire in those grotesque poses are beautiful.

The pastel glow climbs higher and is swallowed up by the cold dull cloudbank. A small flock of sparrowlike birds flutters down and lands erratically just beyond the concertina, chirping and scratching and looking for seeds or worms or insects or whatever it is that small birds look for. After a while one of the nondescript little feathered creatures flies up and alights in the wire beside one of the dead NVA whose arm is thrust skyward as though begging for a handout from Heaven. The feathered head tilts back and lets loose a melodic twittering that rises and falls in the heavy dawning air. A slight smile struggles across my face. Ain't life grand?

Burial detail. We plugged 'em, now we gotta plant 'em. Bitching and cursing and stumbling and more bitching as we struggle to drag the dozen or so bodies from our sector to a small narrow gully fifty or sixty meters below the wire. Little bastards are a lot heavier than you'd think. Should've just let the buzzards eat 'em, or piled 'em up and doused 'em with diesel fuel and made a gook bonfire, but no, the brass says we gotta bury this shit. Don't see one fucking officer humping a gook or carrying an E-tool. Shit.

Early afternoon sun glares through a rare break in the clouds high overhead as we dump our grisly burdens in a careless heap at the edge of the shallow ravine. Several of us grab E-tools and drop into the depression and begin fighting the rocky earth, while others spread out and stand guard. I dig for fifteen or twenty minutes in the unseasonable heat, then Hoppy jumps down to relieve me. I climb out of the deepening trench, wiping stinging sweat from my eyes with a dirty sleeve. Walk to a point just above the carcass pile and sit my weary young ass down on a moss-covered rock.

Looking out across the expanse of valley to the river below, winding like a silvery ribbon at the foot of the high ridges that rise like a foreboding black wall beyond. A fortress of rocks and caves and tangled jungle and gooks. Damn them. Mortars and rockets and artillery and air strikes and napalm and *still* the bastards crawl out of those hills like piss ants to hit us and harass us and make life generally miserable. Sometimes you can see 'em moving around up there in broad daylight. Fucking hard-core bastards have got balls, all right. Big brass ones.

I suddenly sense how exposed I am, sitting here on my rock and leaning back against this bush. Sniper could be taking aim right now. Aligning the crosshairs, breathing out and holding it; slowly taking out the trigger slack with a careful, steady squeeze . . . fuck it. I'm too goddamn tired to give a shit anymore. Go ahead, gook—put one through my running lights. I dare you.

The grave is finished. Filthy, sweat-drenched Marines scramble out of the waist-deep final resting place, seeking a brief respite of shade and a quick drink of tepid water or purple Kool-Aid from green plastic canteens. Those of us who have been standing watch lay down our weapons and walk over to the pile of bodies that have already begun to bloat and stiffen from the unusual break in the winter monsoon.

I look down at the human waste pile. A huge mass of flies rises in agitated swarms at our approach, buzzing in a thousand different directions, then alights again to feast upon the booty of gore. It strikes me that this display of degradated humanity, this awful pile of blood and guts and bones and brains and flesh and shit, doesn't bother me at all. To me, they are not even human. I've felt more pity and compassion for possums killed along the roads back home. I remember how my dog Porkey got run over by that semi when I was twelve, and how torn-up I was, and how I cried and grieved for weeks. I remember how I used to hunt squirrels with my friend Dave, and how sometimes we would only wound one and have to finish it off, how I always felt a certain amount of pity and remorse for the furry little things, even though we were hunting them for food. But I feel nothing for the pile of stinking garbage I see before me now.

That sickly-sweet, thick, shitty smell—not unlike rotted shrimp shells left too long in the July sun—smacks us in the face; the kind of stink you can almost taste, that clings to clothes and skin and hair and doesn't want to go away for days afterward. I don't feel a goddamn bit sorry for the gook whose midsection has been blown away, and whose backbone juts out in morbid, obscene angles; or the gook whose intestines are strung out like putrid sausage links a dozen feet from the stinking stack; or the gook whose face no longer exists, except for a piece of lower jaw with shattered teeth.

We grab the bodies by the handiest stiffened arm or leg, and fling them unceremoniously into the pit to the sound and stench of protesting farts emitted from assholes and mouths and gaping wounds. We deplete the pile, but the flies continue to congregate on the pools of black cherry Jell-O blood which remain. A dozen E-tools heap showers of red earth and rocks upon the mass grave, until only a wayward jutting hand or foot remain above the surface. A couple of impatient undertakers jump down and quickly stomp the uncooperative limbs into compliance.

Job done. Ceremony over. Ashes to ashes, dust to dust. Better these gooks, than any of us.

22

Just got back in from a short, squad-size patrol. Saw nothing except a flock of pheasants that we flushed out of a grassy area. We were moving slow and easy, just waiting for the gooks to hit us at any time, when the birds exploded almost at our feet and took off on whirring wing beats for maybe fifty meters before disappearing in the tall grass. Scared us shitless. Thought we'd bought the farm for sure. Swallowed our hearts and moved on. Beautiful damn birds, something like ringneck pheasants except they were an iridescent, burnished gold color. Made me think about hunting quail back home. This valley would be a great place to hunt if there wasn't a war going on and you didn't have to worry about getting killed all the time.

Passed our last checkpoint and were headed back when we heard the tubes. Scrambled for any pitiful cover we could find and waited for the pounding, just knowing we'd been caught out in the open with our pants down. After the first couple of rounds landed, we realized they were hitting the company area. In a sick sort of way we were glad we were out humping it on patrol.

Got closer to our lines and saw a chopper coming in, so we figured the company took casualties. Felt bad and anxious about that, wondering who it might be. Practically ran the last couple of hundred meters back to the wire. One of the tanks parked just off the road took a hit, and the whole crew was wounded. Somebody said they heard that one of the tank's own rounds blew. Don't know if they were trying to shoot back at the gooks, or if the incoming set off the round. Doesn't really matter. They're all messed up pretty bad, and one of our tanks has been knocked out. Doc Poteat says he thinks they'll all make it, though.

I wait for dark, then I take my E-tool and feel my way through the bushes behind our fighting holes. Gaining some night vision now, so I scrape out a small depression, lower my trousers and squat over the hole. A sickening gurgle rumbles through my bowels as they explode, sending the blackish, stinking spray far beyond the confines of my slit-trench. Jesus, not again . . . I've had the shits on and off for nearly two weeks now. Mostly on. Probably just a stomach virus, Doc says. Not much fever. Damn . . . here it comes again. My insides wretch and my asshole reverberates with motorboat farts as I squirt what must be a quart of the liquid shit into the hole. It takes a whole pack of C-ration shit paper to wipe the foul spray off the cheeks and crack of my ass.

I pull my trousers up and retie my improvised bandolier strap-belt. Losing more weight. Then I scrape as much of the violated earth as I can back into the hole, but

I know my efforts are largely futile, like an inexperienced kitten covering its first few piles. Damn blowflies'll have a field day here tomorrow.

I find a stick on the ground and wallow it around in the hole until the end is covered with a thick coating of shitty mud. I push up my left sleeve, exposing the festering cut on my wrist I got while stringing wire. Grit my teeth and jab at the wound, scraping off the scab. Rub the putrid poultice back and forth into the deep scratch. Wipe off the excess and lower my sleeve.

There. That oughta do it for sure. Damn thing's been infected for a week. Showed it to Doc Hamm, hoping I might get out of the bush for a couple of days. Visions of clean sheets, hot showers and real chow dancing through my head. No such luck. Doc just gave me some penicillin tabs and said it oughta clear up in a few days. Well, fuck that shit. Threw 'em away. Been treating the cut myself with my special remedy for several days. If I can get some red streaks started up my arm, Doc'll have to send me to Delta Med for treatment. Fucking-A! A few more days of Dr. Mikey's Magic Medicine, and I'll be out of here for sure. I think I can hack a few days of bed rest and nurses.

This is a very bad day. The mountain ridges around us lie hidden in the shroud of black clouds that drifts through the valley like the Angel of Death. Heavy mist drips like blood and tears from every bush and tree on our miserable knoll. A few feet away, I chance another glance from the corner of my eye at the corpsmen working frantically, trying to save the lieutenant FO, but he's been shot through the neck and chest and has already turned pallor-gray. They know and I know that they are losing, but they keep on trying anyway, so they can at least keep busy instead of just standing around and watching him go through his death throes.

The lieutenant begins twitching and gulping, like a fish thrashing on the bottom of a boat. I can hear the throaty rattle of death they always seem to make when they die hard, and one of the docs is screaming at the FO, pounding on his bloody chest and Jesus H. Christ Doc, just stop it and let him fucking die, won't you please?

I turn away. Farther down the slope, the survivors of third platoon sit around the seven or eight poncho-covered bodies, staring or crying or trying to console each other. Nearby, other corpsmen are busy changing battle dressings or checking medevac tags for proper information on the wounded.

A chopper lands, and then another, and just like that they are gone with the wounded, but the corpses remain to taunt us and haunt us with exposed boots or arms or tops of heads. They scream at us that just a short hour ago they were one of us, young and living and breathing and full of piss and vinegar and hopes and dreams. They cry out that they want to be with us again, but they can't; they have passed on to that select group to be hosed down, embalmed and bagged by graves registration. Heading home in their handsome silver coffins and star-spangled banners to be King of the Block for a day. Heroes of the obituary columns. Maybe even a picture and story on the front page of the *Hometown Crier,* and boy, won't our families and friends and girls cry and carry on and we'll be the talk of the town for a while. And then they'll lower us away and twenty-one guns and "Taps" and a bronze marker to tell all the world that we once were.

But you poor bastards have to stay behind in this god-forsaken place and bitch and curse and hump and fight and kill and bleed and be wet and cold and hot and sick and hungry and miserable and homesick and all those wonderful things that good grunts do so well until you meet that special round with your name on it and you buy the farm and join us too.

The corpsmen have finally given up on the FO. They stand around, smoking, looking helpless and tired. Nobody speaks. What would they say, anyway? A gust of wet wind catches the upper corner of the poncho and it flips over, fluttering like a waving flag. I find myself staring at the now lifeless face, mouth agape, eyes open and staring nowhere. Strawberry blond hair matted brown with blood. Saint Christopher medal and tiny gold cross lying haphazardly on the ground beside the face, chain still encircling the shattered neck.

The sky grows even darker, and it begins to rain. I find Beard and Larson, and we head down the hill toward our hooch and a miserable night.

Resupply chopper today brought us out a special treat. Along with our mail and the usual cases of C-rations and ammo and water cans, there were fresh baked loaves of bread, thick slices of delicious bologna, and a bag of onions! Chowed down until we were about to bust on triple-decker bologna and onion sandwiches. Each squad got at least two extra bags of onions. That'll dress up our Cs for days to come.

Morton got called up to the company CP this evening. Came back a few minutes later, looking stunned. Bad news from home. His younger brother got killed, gunned down in a street fight or something. Ain't that some weird shit? Chuck's over here fighting this stinking war, and his brother gets blown away back in the World. Nothing seems to make sense anymore.

Doc Poteat gave him something to help him sleep. He'll leave tomorrow and probably be gone about ten days or so. Everybody feels real bad for him. Made us all feel homesick again, and gives us one more thing to carry around and worry about.

Asshole tightening time again. Our squad's got a long patrol and ambush today. Supposed to pass through the area where the third platoon squad got wiped out, then on down to the river and set up an ambush for the night. Sure as hell won't be bored on this hump.

I don't like this shit one bit. A squad's too damn few people to send out around here anymore, even with the gun team we're taking. Whole damn company oughta be going, and even then I wouldn't feel very safe. Not in this valley. Guess the higher-ups think we'll be okay because they've sent a K-9 handler and his German shepherd to go with us on this one. I don't know . . . Rin Tin Tin doesn't look very interested, and his sergeant buddy doesn't seem to be enthusiastic at all.

We leave the wire with Rinny and Sarge up on point with Banks, and begin winding our way farther and farther into the valley. High above the ridges to the north, a tiny observation plane is making one of its daily passes, spotting and plotting targets. The high-pitched buzzing whine of its little engine is drowned out by the thunderous whumping of a CH-53 Sea Stallion beating its way westward toward Khe Sanh, a huge cargo net full of supplies and ammunition suspended below the big chopper. We halt momentarily for the noise to subside, then continue on.

Been at it for an hour now. Excruciatingly slow pace. Senses and nerves on edge and in pain. Terrain has become more rocky, the vegetation stunted and sparse. Getting close to where that squad bought it, but at least we're taking a different route to get there. Garcia checks his map again; points up ahead. We increase our intervals and force ourselves forward. Banks and Hoppy and Sarge and Rinny move ever so cautiously to the mouth of a little grassy meadow strewn with boulders and surrounded almost entirely by higher ground with thick brush. A natural amphitheater. Wet black nose twitches and flares as the shepherd sniffs the ground and air. They move into the meadow with agonizing slowness, working their way around the left side of the open arena. Sweaty palms and tight throats. Please, please don't let 'em hit the shit because if they do we'll have to go get 'em and I sure as shit don't wanna go in there. . . .

A few minutes creep by, then we get the signal to move up. Jesus! How could those guys have been stupid enough to walk through this place? I know there were several new guys in that squad, but the squad leader damn well should've known better. Classic ambush site. Somebody sure fucked up, big-time. . . . Better not pass judgment on 'em. . . . Squad leader probably called and reported what was up. Damn brass probably ordered 'em through. Maybe the squad lead *did* just fuck up . . . might've had his mind on something else. Maybe he found out Jody was banging his girlfriend back home or something.

We search the killing ground and the surrounding high area and find nothing but a lot of spent brass. We take ten to rest and chow down, but I can't eat. Saddle up and move on.

Standing among huge boulders that skirt the river, thirty meters away. The river rushes in rhythmic beauty over its colored rock bed, tumbling and spraying in sparkling cascades, singing the soothing song of nature that only running water and blowing wind can create. On the far side, mossy rocks jut from a higher, steeper bank covered with lush ferns and other rich greenery. I look up and the ridges, black now in the waning light, stand like giants before me. For a few seconds I'm lost in the spectacle. God, what a beautiful place! I could camp here for a month. Reality slaps me in the face, and I remember the danger and death this Shangri-la poses.

We wait for pitch darkness, then carefully stumble and clatter until we're at the river's very edge. Garcia strings us out along the rocky bank facing back the way we came, our backs to the river and the mountains and thousands of gooks. Hold it . . . wait just a damned minute here. You're not *serious*—we're not gonna set up our ambush *here,* are we? You've gotta be out of your mind to set-in here! Our backs to the river and the high ground beyond that's home to a division of NVA and this fucking river screaming in our ears so loud we can't hear shit and no cover except a bunch of rocks that are barely big enough to hide behind if you lie flat this is asking for it this is fucking suicide if we get hit who's gonna save our young asses Rin Tin Tin over there who looks like he's already asleep? Shit. This is *crazy!*

I whisper my opinion and protests to Banks, who's lying a few feet to my right. Maybe we can talk some sense into Garcia, who's obviously recently gone dinky dao, and convince him to move the ambush to a more reasonable site. Banks whispers back, sort of sternly, to just be quiet and take it easy, and that I must be losing my nerve because I've been so jumpy lately.

Jesus H. Christ—I can't *believe* he said that shit to me. That pisses me off and hurts my feelings. What the shit has Banks been doing—taking lifer pills every morning or something? Losing my nerve? *Fuck him!* I don't think a suicidal position is a smart place for an ambush, so that means I'm "losing my nerve?" If that's what he thinks, screw him. Screw 'em all. Okay. I'll lie here with you bastards and play this silly game, and if we get hit we'll see if I do my part, and if we all get fucking zapped at least I can have the satisfaction of saying "I told you so!" Shit.

The night passes, long and uneventful, except for strained senses and frayed nerves. Dawning light finally works its way to the river bottom, and we saddle up and move out with tired eyes and aching muscles. Damn rocks.

We head upstream for a hundred meters or so until the point finds an area that promises an easier route back up the valley to our lines. Fairly easy humping this way. Don't want to get careless though, even though we've got Rin Tin Tin the Wonder Dog and his faithful companion with us.

The Chicom grenade arcs in a lazy tumble up and over

the big boulders to our front. Wild scrambling, diving headlong between or behind rocky cover as automatic AK-47 burst *zings* in crazy ricochets among the rocks surrounding us. Banks or Sarge or somebody up front answers with a long spray from his '16. It's over as quickly as it began. Must've just been a couple of scouts or an observation post or something, but it's enough to convince us to get our young asses out of here, most skosh.

A little later Sarge notices Rinny leaving bloody paw prints on the stony ground. Checks him out and finds a small wound in an upper front leg. Probably took a small piece of shrapnel or a rock fragment from that Chicom. Then Sarge feels a burning in his own calf. Blood. Small puncture wound. How about that shit? Purple hearts all around for the K-9 Corps.

Doc Hamm does his thing and we head on up the valley, glad to leave the river far behind.

23

Great clouds of red dust billow upward to mix with the drooping gray overcast as our convoy speeds eastward along Highway 9. Choking coughs and curses echo above the growling engine and whining tires from the sand-bagged bed of the bouncing six-by where our squad sits. I wipe another layer of grime from my eyes, hike my once-green towel farther up over my nose, and continue to stare through squinted eyes at the hostile hills which rise above the winding, pitted road. Jesus, this shit reminds me of them cowboys riding drag on cattle drives in those westerns I used to watch back home on Saturday mornings. Next time I see one of those flicks, I'll damn sure be more sympathetic for the poor drovers in the rear eating all that trail dust. Shit. . . .

Our platoon drew convoy security today for the run to Dong Ha. Twelve miles or so of fun and games. A chance to visit the PX and get a hot meal. Also a good chance of getting our young asses caught in a big-time ambush. Very little of Highway 9 is considered secure these days, and even those areas are questionable. Charlie hits these convoys about as regularly as a hound dog scratches fleas. Pleasant thought.

Loaded up and headed out early this morning. Hardly went any distance at all before the platoon dismounted and spread out along the flanks of the road for security, while minesweepers passed their magic wands in careful arcs over the road ahead of the long column. First squad ahead on left, third squad on the right, and lucky us walking tail-end-charlie, eating everybody's dust. Oh well . . . at least it breaks up the boredom and monotony of our everyday existence below Camp Carroll. Almost anything for a change. . . .

Slowing down, almost to a crawl, as we approach and pass through Golf Company's position. "Hello's" and "how ya doing's" and good natured "fuck you's" and assorted finger gestures being exchanged between Golf and Echo grunts. Beside me, Larson engages in a shouting exchange of greetings and promised goodies for some dudes he went to boot camp and ITR with. Ol' Jack's got a heart of gold. Always sharing his care packages—and he gets the best ones in the whole damn platoon—with us, and doing anything he can for anybody. One all right number one dude if there ever was one. I love the bastard. Me and him and Beard's gotten just about as tight as you dare to get over here . . . too tight, maybe. Like I was with Bentley. Wonder where he is, and how he's doing? Wonder if he's even still alive?

Passing through Golf's eastern perimeter where a side road intersects with Highway 9. Jesus H. Christ—look at *that* shit! Golf's grunts have jammed the upper torso of a gook they killed on the concrete road post which designates Highway 9 and the other road. The grisly guide is clad in a Marine Corps utility jacket and soft cover. One withered arm points down Highway 9 with bony fingers, while the other points at a right angle down the intersecting road. Sunken, hollow sockets leer from beneath the bill of his cover, and his mummified mouth is stretched into a gruesome grin revealing dark, betel nut–stained teeth. Out-fucking-standing! Get some, Golf.

Dong Ha. Headquarters for the Third Marine Division. Same place I spent the better part of a week burning shit and pulling perimeter duty when I first arrived in-country. Where I tried to bullshit Lampley that night when the gooks probed the lines. The "rear." Yeah, right. Except there *is* no rear here in Vietnam, not when rockets and artillery from across the DMZ can come crashing down at any time and blow one's shit to smithereens. But it *does* feel safe and secure to us, considering where we've been.

I don't recognize a damn thing. Nothing. Could it have changed so much in four months? The trucks grind to a stop in front of a long row of sandbagged buildings, and we climb down and stretch our cramped legs. Garcia checks our weapons to make double-sure they're cleared, and then we're on our own for an hour or so while the trucks are being loaded with ammo and Cs and other supplies, and maybe a replacement or two for the trip back down the gauntlet to Camp Carroll.

We wander along the mud-red streets, taking in the sights and sounds of the privileged pogues' and brass's AO, feeling like ducks out of water. Vietnamese civilians diddy-bop about their daily routines, causing us to fight the urge to unsling our weapons and lock and load. Don't trust none of them gooks.

We find the PX and enter the big tin-and-wood-framed building with wide eyes, like kids let loose in a toy store at Christmas time. So much to see and so much to buy and I just can't decide exactly what I want. A few minutes of fruitless mental struggle, and I settle on a couple of paperback books and some candy bars. Screw it. I'll keep on sending all my money home, and by the time I rotate I'll have enough for that car I want, and maybe enough to put down on that sailboat.

Wandering down some company area now, looking for the enlisted men's mess hall. Beard and Larson carry several bags of booty from the PX. Got all mine stuffed in my trouser pockets. Office and supply pogues keep giving us a wide berth whenever we pass them. Act like we got the plague or something. They look so neat and proper in their pressed, clean green utilities, starched covers and shined boots. Fuck them rear-echelons—who do they think they are, avoiding our asses? Must be our breath . . . or maybe it's because we haven't had a shower in over a month. Jesus, I'm starting to get a complex.

I spot a sandbagged tent with a two-foot-long mirror hanging on a support pole just off a narrow side street. Ain't seen myself since we left the ship, so I walk over and take a look. *Jesus H. Christ!* Who is this bedraggled-looking bastard? Can't be *me!* But it is. Dirty, sallowy skin. Sunken eyes that seem to look beyond the reflection and focus nowhere. Grimy cracks and crevices, overgrown with adolescent peach fuzz, like some farmer's unkempt field. My skin bristles, my stomach knots, and I almost recoil at the ogre staring back at me. . . . Jesus, what's *happened* to me? What have I become? Wasn't that long ago when I could walk along the boardwalk at the beach back home with my buddies and the girls would croon and fawn all over us because we looked like surfers and played in a band and lived in good ol' P.C. and wasn't that just too damn much? Shit, they'd probably scream and run the other way now. No wonder those REMFs gave us so much room. I don't recognize this haggard bastard at all. Is this what no sleep and fear and death and killing does? No nineteen-year-old looks like this. No, they look young and innocent and full of life and hope and promise. Not like this ragged, worn-out shell staring back at me. Shit.

Had our hot meal at the mess hall. Spaghetti. Delicious. Ate until we were bloated, then went back for more. Chow down while you've got the chance.

Passed back through Golf Company's lines, and Larson tossed cartons and cartons of cigarettes and candy bars and other shit to his buddies. Olive-drab Santa Claus bringing Christmas in February. Big-hearted bastard spent almost his whole damn paycheck, and gave most of it away. I'm sending mine home to save, as usual. Maybe Larson knows something I don't.

Back on hole watch in the valley. Another hour and I can wake Beard up and get some sleep. Been a long day. A real ass-kicker. Convoy duty is okay though, especially if you don't hit the shit. We skated.

I raise my head above the lip of our hole and take a quick look around. Across the valley the black ridges loom menacingly in the falling darkness. To my left, twenty

meters away, I can barely make out the top of a camou-
flaged helmet cover as one of the Marines in an adjacent
hole does his own anxious peeking toward the enemy-held
high ground. Must be Hoppy or Thompson, or maybe
Gray. I glance to the right toward the other hole where
Garcia and Banks and Warner should be. Nothing. Below
ground, like good little groundhogs.

I squat back down and lean against the cool, earthen
wall. Darkness has flowed into our hole, filling it with
pitch blackness.

"See anything out there yet?" Beard's strange "Down
East" Maine accent cuts the void with his tension-reliev-
ing question.

"Fucking-A. Boo-coo darkness." False bravado reply.
I'm scared shitless, and they know it. They are too. Even
Larson, sitting over there somewhere in this inkwell with
all his big-city cool, hasn't managed to muster up any of
his usual Big Apple bullshit to lay on us this time.

Something big is up. Word came down for everybody to
be in their holes and below ground by 1900 because
they're fixing to pound the shit out of the ridges with a
B-52 strike. Arc Light. Some very serious shit. Moonscape
City. I remember walking through that wasteland near
Con Thien back in December. How the whole platoon
could spread out in one bomb crater with plenty of room
to spare. How nothing seemed to be left alive for hundreds
of meters in all directions. Jesus.

Wonder what's going on? Talked it over with Beard and
Larson a little while ago, and we concluded that the NVA
must be massing for an attack to overrun us and take out
Camp Carroll. Oh, wondrous thought. We ran out of con-

versation just before dark. A bad case of nervous waiting seems to've put a choke hold on our vocal chords. What are we gonna say to each other, anyway?

"Hey, guys, y'all really think several thousand gooks are about to pour out of those mountains and sweep up this valley and annihilate our young asses?"

"Probably so. Seems like a logical thing for them to do at this stage of the game. What do you think?"

"Well, that sounds like a fitting scenario to me. Perhaps we should call for a B-52 bombardment and try to thwart the enemy's plans. That just might prove to be an effective measure for this current situation."

Snap back to reality. Christ—the bullshit that can run through your head when you're scared and waiting for it to happen!

"Hey, Beard. What fucking time is it?"

He mumbles a curse through the darkness about his luminous dial not illuminating, hunches over and strikes his Zippo. Yellow flame chases the black out of our hole, filling it with raging bonfire brightness. Before Larson can finish his whispered yell of "Jesus Christ, blow it the fuck out!" he does, and the night flows back into our hole with blinding relief. Visions of B-52 bombardiers zeroing-in on our glaring signal fire fill my mind with sudden panic, and terror grips me. I fight off the urge to vacate this hole and seek refuge in the next one. Black humor replaces self-induced fear as I remember that the craters from those two-thousand-pounders would reach from hole to hole anyway. I giggle aloud with that close-to-insane giddiness as Beard says, "1925."

1925! Jesus H. Christ—you'd think the brass could get

their shit together for once and do something according to schedule, but no, they can't even drop their fucking bombs on time. Hurry up and wait. Bullshit as usual. Probably gonna call the whole thing off anyw—

Tremendous white flash blows the darkness out of the sky and bass drums are pounding in both ears and the ground is shaking and vibrating must be an earthquake this hole is gonna open up and swallow us dirt is flying all around and my ears oh my ears hands clamped over them squeezing tight but the lightning keeps flashing and thunder keeps crashing inside my head and we're bouncing off the floor and against the walls of this grave and it hurts it hurts so loud so loud go away go away on our knees and elbows pray pray if you can for it to stop so loud god the noise is a sledgehammer bludgeoning us nearly senseless this is crazy how can the gooks stand this so loud so loud it hurts jaws ache they can't stand it they just die and get buried and disintegrate into thin air and ashes and shit gotta stop can't go on knocked senseless at football practice head-on tackling drills really do see stars ammonia sticks yeah somebody bust an ammonia stick up my nose and chase this hurt and noise and stars away. . . .

The ground quits quaking and the night slips out of its hiding place to blanket our world again. It's over. High-pitched, electroniclike ringing fills my ears, and a terrible buzzing hums through my aching head. Larson says something to me, but I can't hear him and shake my head to try and clear it. Something warm and wet runs down my right jaw and cheek and onto my neck. Blood? I fumble for a match and strike it. I wipe at the fluid oozing from my ear and check my fingers in the dancing glow of the match. Clear. Not bloody. That's a relief. Had me worried there for a minute. Probably just my brains leaking out or something.

The match dies and we sit in the darkness, waiting as the ringing slowly diminishes and our hearing gradually returns. Like punch-drunk fighters collapsed in their corners, we think very little and say even less. Full alert until twenty-two hundred, if you can call it that. Too dark to see, and our hearing is shot to shit. Beard checks the time and takes the first watch.

24

God, what a beautiful sight. Early morning sun glares from the southeastern sky and shatters the usual dull blanket into clouds of billowy marshmallows and reflective steel wool, accented by scattered patches of deep winter blue. Far to the northwest, past the ridges which encircle our valley, filtered rays strike jagged rocky mountaintops, setting them ablaze in dazzling hues of burnished gold, reddish-orange and purple. Landscape artist's dream.

Walking down the road from Camp Carroll, back to our position on the knoll. The higher elevation and clearing sky combine to give us the breathtaking vista and the promise of a beautiful day. A far cry from last night's ambush, spent shivering in a chilling drizzle, huddled together for body heat where we lay hidden in tall elephant grass two hundred meters east of Camp Carroll. Miserable, sleepless night.

A convoy is forming for the run to Dong Ha. Two dozen or more six-bys are strung out along the road, interspersed with jeeps armed with pedestal-mounted machine guns, and a couple of balloon-tired "mules" sporting 106mm recoilless rifles. Bored crews doze in the warming sun, or methodically clean weapons or double-check gear. Security platoon is spread out off both sides of the road in long columns, so we relax our guard and stroll along, talking in twos or threes, like a casual walk in the park.

Walking abreast with Beard and Larson, talking about hometowns and dreams and plans for the future when we rotate back to the World. We figure we'll all be stationed at Camp Lejeune when we get back, so we plan on "swooping" to each other's hometowns on long weekends. Playing Chamber of Commerce advocates, each touting the attractions and adventures that await us in *our* little niche of the World. Friendly arguments and bullshit flowing so deep now that it threatens to flow over our boot tops.

Yeah, right, Beard . . . but what do we do after we see the apple orchards and potato fields? Go lobstering maybe, or moose hunting? Shit. Bet the broads up in Maine are as cold as the weather. What do y'all do for excitement up there, rub noses? I'll bet the women up there look real sexy, wrapped up in those parkas and mufflers and earmuffs and shit.

Sure, Larson . . . So, you're gonna show ol' Beard and me the Big Apple, huh? Gonna take us to all them fancy nightclubs where everybody knows you because you're so cool and popular and dance like Fred Astaire. Gonna introduce us to those big-city sophisticated women of the world who'll show us small town country hicks what *real* loving is and all that good shit. Sounds real exciting. But, tell me,

Jack, how much do they charge—as much as the ones in Tijuana—and do they really braid their armpit hair and wear coin-changers around their waists and all have the clap?

Hey, *Florida's* where it's at, guys. This ain't no bull-shit—the sand on our beaches looks just like sugar, and the water is blue-green and clear, and the climate is warm and the broads flock to the beach from all over the South in the summer—more broads than you can shake your stick at. And y'all *know* what they say about Southern women, don't you? Well, it's all true! I swear, they're as thick as flies lying on the beach, all covered with good-smelling suntan lotion and not much else, and a lot of 'em undo their tops while they sunbathe, and sometimes they doze off and forget about it and roll over or sit up and Jesus, what a sight! Y'all Yankees just wouldn't believe it, but it's the truth, I swear, no bullshit.

Mid-afternoon. Supply chopper's in. Garcia sends half the squad up to the LZ to get our ammo, C-rats and water cans, along with any mail that may have come in for the squad. Me and Warner struggle down the slope with two five-gallon water cans apiece that must weigh fifty pounds each when full. These are definitely filled to the brim. Shit. Banks and Hoppy follow behind us, each humping a couple of cases of Cs. Off to my left I see Lance Corporal Hubbard, from first squad. Hubbard's the biggest man in the whole company. Probably six-foot-six, and must weigh about two-thirty or forty. All muscle, as strong as an ox. Country boy from Mississippi. Bet his mama had a hard time keeping him full. Looks like he could eat a whole damn case of Cs at one sitting. A real nice dude, though, the gentle-giant type. I look in awe as he strolls along, as easy as you please, whistling what sounds like a church hymn, two heavy water cans clenched in each huge fist. Jesus.

Late afternoon. Garcia informs me that I've got the LP again tonight. Fuck this shit. Ambush last night, and now a goddamn LP. Haven't slept in two days. Must think we're machines or something. I guess we are—little cogs in the great big Green Machine. Can't take too much more of this shit. Gotta have a break or I'm gonna fucking lose it. So damn tired of patrols and ambushes and working parties and hole-watch and LPs and the shit never lets up. I think I'm going crazy sometimes. I think we're *all* going crazy. How much of this shit do they think we can *take?* I'm so damn tired of it all. Never stops. Either getting shot at or fucked with or dodging incoming. Never get enough sleep, and I haven't had my boots off in over a week . . . feet are probably rotted away . . . toes will probably come off with my socks. Shit.

Raining again. Wonderful. Fits my mood. Oh well, it'll be dark in less than two hours. I hunch my shoulders against the cold drizzle and head out into the gloom to find Beard and Thompson and give them the good news.

Inside the hooch, getting ready to chow down before we have to leave for the LP. Beard sits to my left with his legs tucked under him, carefully heating the chicken and noodles I traded him on our improvised C-ration can stove. Bastard loves that shit. Hoards chicken and noodles like it was gold, and he was King Midas.

To Beard's left, Larson is cleaning his field-stripped M-14, scrubbing the parts with his toothbrush and gun oil. Gray reclines against the wall to my right, his head propped up on his folded flak jacket, reading a fuck book. I sit cross-legged, Indian-fashion, staring at the layer of grease floating on top of the beans and franks I'm eating cold. Hardly ever heat my Cs anymore. Why bother? Tastes the same anyway.

I scoop another glob of peanut butter from the small tin with my plastic spoon and spread it on a John Wayne cracker. Been eating a lot of this stuff lately, hoping to slow down my case of the shits. Not working yet.

Gray lets loose a long, low whistle as he turns a page in his book; reaches down to scratch his crotch. Either his jungle rot's bothering him, or he's playing with himself. Must be a good book. Beard stirs the simmering white blob of noodles laced with tiny specks of pinkish-brown meat, samples a spoonful and stirs some more. I tell him to hurry up because we gotta get going in a few minutes, just as Thompson enters the hootch, water dripping from a thousand rivulets off his helmet and poncho. He looks pissed. He's been out trying to talk Hoppy or Warner into taking his place on the LP tonight. Obviously struck out.

"What'sa matter, pussy? Couldn't sucker anybody into taking your place?" Beard says, half-jokingly, as he methodically stirs the chicken and noodles.

"Shut your fucking mouth, Beard, before I blow you away!" Thompson snaps back angrily, agitation spread across his face like a mask.

Beard chuckles and nods his head up and down, mockingly. "Sure, sure," he says in that strange giggly manner of his. Looks up smiling and locks eyes with Thompson. "You ain't got the *balls* to blow anybody away!"

Thompson stands framed in the hatchway of the hooch for a few strained seconds, then he yells, "I'll blow *your* fucking ass away!"

Larson looks up from cleaning his rifle, and Gray puts down his book. I still think they must just be messing with each other—hell, Beard's always fucking around and joking with everybody; that's just his way. The class clown. Everybody knows that. But the joke's over because Thompson flips his poncho aside and reaches down and grips the operating rod of his M-16, pulls it back and releases it, chambering a round and *whoa there, Thompson, that's enough this shit ain't funny anymore just what the fuck do you think you're doing oh Jesus no! Don't point the fucking weapon Thompson don't fuck around like that asshole don't fucking point the weap—*

Pop! Muffled report as the '16 explodes and Beard is slammed flat on his back as if struck by a freight train, legs bent under his body. Thompson drops the rifle, jumping up and down like he's running in place, crying and screaming incoherently. Beard bounces up crazily on his knees, teetering back and forth and side to side like a jack-in-the-box, hands clutched over his heart and a wild look of shocked surprise and disbelief on his face.

I am horrified and utterly helpless as our eyes meet and his stare screams out at me for help. And then the stare fades and the eyes roll back until there's only white filling the sockets and an awful, wrenching, guttural *"Uuugghhh!"*

rises from his chest and up his throat and out of his mouth to pierce my ears and mind and heart and soul and I'm up and out of the hooch and running down the lines screaming *"Corpsman up! Corpsman up! Corpsman up!"* and I'm past our lines and still running running running away from the sight and the sound and the horror of it all, but I can't escape. I'm on my knees and pounding the ground with clenched fists and raising my hands toward Heaven and pleading, *"God, God, not Beard, oh God no, not Beard, take me take me take me!"*

Walking back toward our area now, totally drained. I pass near the platoon CP, and I see Doc Poteat and Doc Hamm working frantically on the limp, unresponsive body. Blood covers the bare chest, and from the bloody appearance of the lower throat I know they've trached him. But he's horribly gray like the lieutenant FO and so many others and I know that it's no use. I wander on down past our positions, and Corporal Shuster from first squad puts his arm around my shoulders and sets me down on the sandbags lining one of his squad's fighting holes. Doesn't say anything, or if he does, I don't hear it; but he's there, and that's what counts. . . .

Long minutes pass. Nearly dark now, so I get up and walk back in the direction of our hooch, not really knowing where to go or what to do, and not really caring. Larson's walking toward me.

"How is he?" I manage weakly, not really wanting to hear what I already know.

"How is *who?*" he snaps back, the slapping anger in his voice taking me by surprise.

"Beard." The name cracks in my throat.

"Beard's fucking *dead!*" Larson says, and walks away into the deepening shadows.

Up the hill we trudge toward Camp Carroll, in a long, slow-moving column. Don't know how many days it's been since Beard died. A week, maybe. Don't know or remember much of anything anymore. Don't really care. It don't mean shit. Nothing means shit anymore. Leaving this godforsaken valley and part of myself behind. Forever.

Another long column of bedraggled grunts passes us as they head down the road to take up our old positions on the knoll. Our relief. Nobody says a word. Jesus . . . They look as bad as we do. But it don't mean shit, because they're just like us. Leaving one Hell behind, and heading for another.

25

The amtracks plow through the river like a flotilla of lumbering green sea turtles, muddy water boiling up in the wake of the churning tracks. We sit stoically on layers of sandbags atop the laboring landing craft, paying little heed to the singing and snapping of sporadic small-arms fire passing overhead. Nowhere to hide, so fuck it. Don't do much good to duck, anyway. When your number comes up, you're gone. There it is.

Scoop is the NVA has moved a large force into the area north of the Cua Viet River, and are building fortified bunkers and positions in several of the small villages in there. Convoys of supply boats have been getting hit hard as they ferry supplies up the river to Dong Ha from the sea. Could be massing for an attack on Division Headquarters at Dong Ha a little southwest of here. Our job is to find 'em and kill 'em, or drive 'em back across the DMZ. The battalion we're relieving got chewed up pretty bad. I think this is going to be some serious shit.

I glance over my right shoulder across the wide river

and see several other amtracks crowded with Marines plodding through the choppy waters, their mud-stained helmet covers looking like a forest of toadstools on a floating island. My ass begins to go numb from sitting in one position too long, so I struggle to a knee and sit with one cheek resting on my flexed foot. Steady breeze blows warm in our faces, then suddenly grows cool, then warm again. My ankle aches and my toes burn from rot, so I sit back down on my ass again. Close my eyes and listen to the droning of the engines, the vibration lulling me almost to sleep.

Jolted awake as the treads dig into the low, irregular river bank, and the amtrack lumbers ashore like an ungainly walrus. Quickly, we jump down and spread out as other 'tracks come ashore here and there, deposit their loads, and slip back into the water heading for the far shore, like creatures performing an ancient, instinctive ritual.

I look around the new surroundings. Nothing like the jungled mountains of Camp Carroll. Dirty white sand dunes dotted with sparse, low-growing vegetation roll on and on as far as I can see. In the distance, an area of taller trees and lusher greenery stands out like an oasis in the sea of sand. I think I can make out a few thatched rooftops. Must be a vill. Wonder if it's friendly, or one of those the NVA's turned into a fortress?

Overcast sky hangs low and threatening, culminating in angry blue-black clouds rolling on the horizon to the north that contrast in eerie beauty with the white dunes and flats. Far away, Mother Nature beats thunder from her bass drums, and white-hot jags of lightning dance against the clouds like a chain of diamonds in a coal bin. An illusion of black and white beauty that can reach down without warning and strike you dead. Death in disguise, like this whole goddamn country.

We move out.

The village is ours. Took two tries to take it, but it's ours. As Banks digs, I sit exhausted at one end of the unfinished fighting hole, looking toward another cluster of trees and hooches in the distance. My legs dangle in the hole, and I spin the handle of my E-tool around and around between the insteps of my boots. Wonder if the gooks are there, too? Might be. Sure di-di'd out of here fast, once we broke through.

Twenty meters to my right, Hoppy and Warner are methodically digging another hole. Jesus, Hoppy sure looks pale without a shirt. Indian-red arms and ghost-white body. Everybody else turns brown. Not ol' Hoppy. He just gets red. Don't see Larson or Garcia or Morton. Wonder where they're at? Probably at the CP.

I slip back into the hole and resume digging. Real easy digging here, not like on the knoll below Camp Carroll. Goddamn rocks and sticky red clay you had to scrape off the blade after each shovelful. This sandy shit is a skate. . . .

Strange, but I can't remember very much about the firefight for the vill. . . . I know they shelled the shit out of this place for hours last night, and then the phantoms swooping in with the napalm this morning, and then we're charging across this wide open area again that must've been five hundred meters across and I never thought we'd make it with the mortars and artillery and

rockets crashing down and the rounds Jesus the rounds
thick as flies buzzing and cracking everywhere and little
sand geysers erupting all around and we just ran and ran
so slow though God it was so slow through all that loose
sand and screaming and hollering and cracking and popping and keep going keep going gotta get across in the
tree line get in the tree line and kick the gooks' asses out
of there yeah kick them out of the trees and the trenches
and the holes and through the vill and out the other side
and then the vill is ours. . . .

We find a body near the ruins of a hooch behind our
hole. This fucker is truly wasted . . . napalm's done turned
him into a genuine crispy critter. We stare in fascination
at the blackened corpse. Ears burned away completely.
Nose burned off so there's just some charred bone with
nasal holes. Lips melted away, revealing blistered gums
and stained teeth locked in a hideous grin. One eye socket
burned hollow, the other sporting what looks like a large
yellow blister rising a couple of inches out of the skull.
Fingers and toes all reduced to black nubs. Balls and dick
gone, except for a blackened half-inch stub—never gonna
please ol' mama-san with that little thing. But the coup de
grace is the toasted section of intestine that rises from the
split abdomen and balloons upward for six or eight inches.
Golden-brown and crispy looking, just like the yellow bubbles that rise up on the skin of barbequing chicken. Ain't
this some shit . . . ain't this some fascinating shit?

Somebody finds a rope, and we loop it under his out-
stretched arms and around his body and string him up on
a post still standing from the blown-away hooch behind
our hole. Shit, this is better than that half-a-gook Golf

Company had sitting on that road post. Here you go gooks. Use this for an aiming point. Hit it if you can, you slope-headed sons of bitches. We dare you. You gook motherfuckers can't hit shit. . . .

We've named our new neighbor "Charcoal Charlie." Getting dark now, so we man our holes in case some of Charlie's buddies decide to come visit during the night. We open our Cs and chow down as the shadows lengthen and the night falls. We watch Charcoal Charlie hanging from his pole, staring out over the open expanse toward the next village with his yellow-blister eye, until he blends in and disappears into the black.

Got me some number-one souvenirs today. We moved out early and hid behind some dunes until the barrage lifted, then we swept the vill. It was a big village, but resistance was light. No incoming like there usually is. Most of the gooks were either dead or had hauled ass.

Checked out a big stucco building that had been mostly destroyed by air strikes. Two damaged walls and part of the roof were all that was left standing. Turned out to be a schoolhouse, probably built by the French. Books and papers scattered everywhere amid overturned tables, chairs, desks, bookcases and other debris. Always did like books, so I rummaged through the wreckage to see what I could find. Found a copy of *Rip Van Winkle* with columns printed side-by-side in Vietnamese and English, and a small dictionary translating Vietnamese into English words or phrases. Also found several books and pamphlets on different subjects, but by this time Garcia was yelling at us to move out, so I crammed as much as I could into my pockets.

We moved up a slope where a group of hooches, or what was left of 'em, stood among a grove of trees. Started checking out the hooches for gooks or bodies or weapons. Inside one, I saw a table in a corner near a window. There was a clay bowl with a melted candle sitting on the table, and underneath was something bundled up in a little blanket. Checked it out for wires, then I drug it out with the barrel of my rifle. Heard something rattle like dishes, so I figured it wasn't gonna blow up in my face. Unfolded the blanket and there it was—a beautiful tea set. Must've been my karma, or something. A tea set for ol' Teapot! Looks like real bone china, ivory-colored with delicate inlaid etchings in blue, of pagodas and exotic birds like peacocks and pheasants. Four delicate cups and saucers, a sugar bowl, creamer and teapot. Couldn't believe my luck, finding something so beautiful and fragile and unscathed amid this world of violence and destruction.

I carefully wrapped it back up in the blanket and placed the small bundle in a cloth sack I found in the hooch. Knotted it under my cartridge belt against my left hip, and carried it around like a sack of eggs until we got back to our position late this evening. Tore pages from the pamphlets I found earlier, wadded 'em up and placed 'em between the individual pieces. Then I stacked the pieces inside a pair of socks, tied 'em off, and laid 'em in my pack, using the sack and blanket for cushioning.

Won't be much of a problem to mail *Rip Van Winkle* and the dictionary home. But the tea set is another story. Gonna have to hump it around until I can get to Dong Ha or someplace to pack and mail it. It'll be worth it, though.

Now all I gotta do is figure out where I'm gonna carry my extra gear and Cs.

Took another village built alongside the river this morning. Scoop is, we'll be operating out of this one for a while, so we dug-in deep.

Captured myself a prisoner after we'd kicked the NVA out of the vill—a gook chicken. Saw him trying to sneak away, so I alerted the rest of the squad and we surrounded him. He refused to surrender, so we moved in. I intercepted his frantic dash for freedom with a diving tackle, catching him by a flapping wing, sending feathers and cackles flying. We held a summary court-martial, found him guilty of being a communist sympathizer by unanimous vote, and sentenced him to death. Sentence was immediately carried out by Hoppy, who wrung its scrawny little neck. I built a small fire while Warner and Banks plucked and cleaned the unfortunate fowl. Then we roasted it on a spit over coals, basting it with C-ration pineapple jam. Just got a little piece each, but it sure tasted good.

No resupply yet, and everybody's low on water, so me and Warner gather up the squad's canteens and head across the vill to the river. Warner stands guard while I kneel beside some bushes growing along the bank and submerge the first two canteens into the murky water, being careful not to disturb the silty bottom. Shit's kinda muddy, but at least it's wet. Be surprised at how unparticular you can be when you're really thirsty. Tried to spice up my can of pork slices the other night with black pepper. Overdid it. Jesus, I thought I was gonna die! Drained what was left from both my canteens, then went all around the platoon begging a little water here and there. Never gonna do that shit again.

I finish filling the canteens. We string 'em together with bandolier straps and sling 'em over our shoulders and head back. Somewhere near the middle of the vill I stumble over something and barely manage to catch myself from falling flat on my face. I look back to see what I tripped over. Jesus!

"Hey, Warner . . . look at this shit!" I work the toe of my boot under the loose dirt and leaves from which the stump of a leg protrudes, and with a grunt flip the body out of the shallow grave. It lands face-down, so I kick it again to roll it over. Dead NVA. Shredded uniform stained almost earthen-color. One leg blown off above the knee. Gaping vertical hole in the chest, and another in the forehead above the left eye. Arty or air-strike did him in, I guess. Been dead for a while, looks sort of mummified. Already bloated and deflated and dried up. No maggots . . . I don't even notice a smell. We check the pockets and find nothing to souvenir, so we kick him back into his grave, pick up the canteens and walk back to our position.

Another day, another village. How many days? I don't know. How many vills? Not sure of that, either. Fucking lost track. It don't mean shit anymore . . . same thing, day after day. Move out before daylight and get into position for the assault. Lie down and wait and watch the light show of exploding artillery and then the streams of tracers and fireballs as the Phantoms scream in lower and lower until you're sure they're gonna be consumed by the very havoc they wreak. Then get on-line and move out across the open ground like pawns on a chessboard until the gooks open up and chaos assumes command and then you're running again, running and stumbling and sprawling but you've gotta keep going and keep the sand out of your weapon there's so much sand it's everywhere in everything pick yourself up and go again amid the explosions all around that you barely notice and you know the air is filled with death but you don't hear the rounds anymore like the factory worker who no longer hears the roar of machinery as he works day after day but you feel the searing heat of the round that sucks wind an inch below your throat when you stumble and fall to your hands and knees but you're not scared just fascinated and amazed that you're still alive so you get up and continue your frantic slow-motion dash across the open through the quicksand and into the vill because that's where the gooks are and that's what you're here for. . . .

Crouched down on both knees behind a mound just inside the tree line. Taking heavy fire from a hooch thirty meters to my front. Feel naked and alone. I look around. Several staggered rows of grassy mounds. Must be a graveyard. Scattered tall trees and carpet of unkempt grass dominate this corner of the hamlet, overshadowing the unmarked mounds. Heavy action coming from my left-front. God, *I'm alone* . . . all alone among the dead . . . but now I hear an M-16 popping in my right ear. . . . Banks, good ol' Banks is behind another mound and pumping round after round into the hooch-disguised bunker ahead.

Far to the left several Marines move forward, racing or sneaking to more advantageous positions. I raise myself over the top of the mound and squeeze off a few quick rounds and duck back behind my haven again just as a long stream of blazing tracers fly from somewhere behind me and tear into the hooch. A quick glance and I see Willis and his A-gunner lying prone fifteen meters to my rear pouring hundreds of rounds into the bunker which has us stalemated in this sector of the vill.

The booming of grenades intermingles with the popping and cracking and chattering staccato of small-arms and automatic weapons, but it's all drowned out by the shouts and screams as leaders maneuver their charges and flesh and bone are ripped and seared by hot flying metal. Smoke billows in wavering gray clouds as the hooch over the bunker ignites and crackles and begins to disintegrate in ashy heat waves and dancing flames before our eyes. Up and rushing forward, pins pulled and flinging the grenades toward the opening where the gooks have us pinned and one explosion followed quickly by another and showers of sparks and debris and we stare into the inferno and two are slumped over and one lies sprawled on his back with outspread arms and we spray a few rounds to make sure and move on.

Moving down a wide path between rows of hooches. Shattered trees and ruins and smoke and fire is all around me and threatens to close in and consume me. Everything has become foggy and unreal. Nothing exists anymore except what waits up ahead—a surrealistic tunnel-vision world of horror.

The apparition flows from the thick choking smoke of a burning hootch and materializes on the path ahead of me. A hag of an old woman, gray and wrinkled and worn with age like the crude sack dress of burlap she wears. Gnarled hands clasped together high against her chest beneath the weathered face, head bobbing up and down over narrow hunched shoulders. . . . The Angel of Death come to claim me? . . . An act of prayer? . . . A plea for mercy? . . . Welcome liberating heroes? . . . Is she hiding a grenade in her hands, or? . . .

I'm thinking there's not supposed to be any civilians left around here, and what are we gonna do with her, but Willis steps up beside me and answers my question with a long burst from his M-60 and a strange grin on his baby-face and I watch in horrid fascination as the tracers fly through the old woman as if she wasn't there and then they pick her up and fling her backward and she lies sprawled along the path like some discarded stuffed animal that's lost its stuffing, cut almost in half.

I walk up to the body and look down. No grenade or weapon. Aged eyes stare back at me from the blank wrinkled face. We move on.

Just keep moving and shooting anything you see but don't stop can't stop just walk and shoot and reload and shoot and throw the grenade and blow the hootch blow the bunker in the trench in the trench finish them off shoot shoot make sure they're dead don't stop reload keep moving reload shoot reload shoot anything you see but I can't see good any longer everything's a blur keep moving through the tunnel blow the hootch reload in the trench they're in the trench shoot shoot throw the grenade keep moving don't know anymore don't have to know just act keep moving through the tunnel shoot and reload and keep moving keep moving don't stop don't stop never stop to stop is to die so move move move. . . .

Incoming . . . somebody must've hollered *"Incoming!"* but I don't hear the voice I just know it's coming, coming like it always does . . . always call it in on their own positions when we overrun 'em and they fall back to the next line of trenches or the next vill.

I dive into the trench as the whistles and explosions and hot flying shrapnel and screams fill the air but I'm not afraid don't know fear anymore I should be afraid because fear is healthy fear keeps you alert and alive and I should feel it but I'm beyond fear I try but it has deserted me left me alone so alone doesn't abide in me anymore. . . .

What is this? Something's under me and it ain't dirt . . . dead gook . . . lying on top of a dead fucking gook! Lying in dead-gook mush of blood and guts and splattered meat and bones. Another one up ahead in the trench . . . top of his head is gone, a pinkish cavity where his brain should be stares back at me. Involuntary giggles shake through me. Damn gook's done lost his mind . . . hasn't got a lick of sense . . . not a brain in his head. . . .

Laughing out loud now. Going crazy—fucking dinky dao! Oh god, I'm losing it. What day is it, anyway? Don't even know how we got in this vill . . . can't remember . . . same one as the dead woman, or? But the sky is blue . . . wasn't blue that day, was it? Must be a different vill, but not sure, can't remember . . . god, *I can't remember!*

Out of the trench and walking on-line down a slope. Who the fuck are these guys beside me? Clean and green and fresh-faced . . . baby new guys. Where did they come from, and what are they doing here by me? Not in my squad . . . but if they're not, what the shit are they doing here? Must've come in with that new platoon sergeant we got. That bastard started riding our asses about shaving and bathing and maintaining proper hygiene and military bearing in the field and I damn jumped in his chest and was gonna spread his shit but Warner and Banks pulled me off. Never seen these fuckers, though. Where is everybody . . . Jesus, what're they doing next to me?

Hooches are being blown and torched as we mop up, and one of the clean green new guys pulls the pin from a grenade and tosses it into a hooch and hollers, *"Fire in the hole!"* and hugs the wall like they teach you to do in street fighting back at Geiger, and I'm fascinated and astonished but I don't say anything about this amazing act of stupidity I just flatten myself out and when the explosion comes I look back at the new guy rolling back and forth on the ground all peppered with shrapnel and bleeding red-brown blood all over his new green utilities.

Through the vill now, resting against a tree at the edge. So tired . . . so goddamn tired. Rest. Gotta rest and think some pleasant thoughts to ease my mind and sooth my aching soul. When I get out of here and back to the World I'm . . . when I get back to the World I . . . doesn't work. It doesn't work. Can't see "back to the World" anymore. Doesn't exist. *This* is my World, my reality, my existence. No more going home to Mickey Mouse Fantasy Land. Can't see that far, can't imagine it happening. Not gonna make it . . . no longer a question of *if* I get hit, just *when.* Nobody makes it out of Horror Land anymore, but at least it's *real.* I can see it and touch it and taste it and feel it and smell it. Not like that imaginary place "back home in the

World" bullshit we used to think about and dream about and hope for. Got all we need right here anyway. Free room and board . . . good pay . . . steady job guaranteed for life until we buy the farm and retire forever.

Yellow smoke drifts by. A chopper lands. I watch as they load the new guy and the other wounded and dead aboard. It lifts up on the cooling rotor wash and disappears toward the southwest.

26

Me and Banks are sitting behind our hole, cooking up a C-ration stew. That's where you take all the leftover meals that nobody can stand to eat anymore, and mix 'em all together with hot sauce, salt, pepper and anything else you can scrounge up. Then you heat it in somebody's steel pot over a piece of C-4 until it bubbles like a witch's cauldron, dish it out into empty cans and enjoy. Well, you eat it, anyway. Still tastes like shit, but at least it's a little different than the usual shit.

Been lying around, skating for a couple of days since we last got our asses kicked. Higher-ups have left us pretty much alone, not fucking us over with senseless working parties or other petty-ass bullshit. Just pulling hole watch at night, but hell, that's second nature anyway. Been sacking out in the shade a lot during the day.

Garcia comes back from the squad leaders' meeting and tells us to take off our skates because there's gonna be a big push tomorrow. Then he looks around what's left of his raggedy-ass squad kinda somber-like, pausing briefly at each face, and says that by this time tomorrow some of us probably won't be here.

Great. That's just fucking great. Beard's dead, Thompson's in the brig, poor ol' Gray should be back in the World but he's at Division waiting for the trial. Warner's gone and Hoppy's gone, and the clean green new guy for a day is gone. And now you tell us it's not gonna get any better, it's just gonna get worse. I don't want to hear this shit, I don't need this shit.

That small, hopeful flame of being out of the shit for a while flickers and dies. Dark, sullen mood fills me again, like the approaching dark, as lengthening shadows grow and merge to chase the last glimmer beyond the western horizon.

Garcia tells me I'm up for promotion, and to report to the Company CP for an interview with the Skipper. I don't really feel like going, because what fucking difference will it make whether I die as a private first class or a lance corporal? Ten thousand dollars is ten thousand dollars and what rank you are don't mean shit when you die because dead is dead. Shit. I sling my rifle and head for the CP.

"Sir, PFC Helms reporting as ordered, Sir." Standing outside the CP tent near the center of the vill. I wait for the voice of authority to tell me to enter, then I duck through the folded flaps, march up to the table where the Captain and First Sergeant are seated, and snap to attention, amazed that I can still do this military bullshit since boot camp was forever ago.

The CO looks up from the file of papers spread before him on the table and tells me to "Stand at ease." Shifts the stub of cigar clenched in his teeth and continues shuffling through the papers.

I relax and decide to be bold and blunt when the questions start. Fuck it. What are they gonna do—send me to Vietnam? The Skipper looks up, leans back in his chair and asks me point-blank why I feel I should be promoted to lance corporal.

I clear my throat nervously. "Because, Sir, I've been in the bush for five months, and I know my shit!" There it is, short and succinct, spoken with all the boldness and confidence I can muster. Probably gonna hang me up by the balls now.

The CO smiles, then he turns to the First Sergeant. "You got something for this youngster, Top?" The skipper always calls us "youngsters"—irritates the hell out of me.

The First Sergeant shuffles a few papers of his own. Looks up with that tanned, leathery face of so many seasons and eyes full of wisdom crowned by a faded soft cover on the short, gray-flecked hair. "Helms, it says here you used to be a clerk-typist, 0141."

"Yessir, Top. For a few months back at Lejeune before I changed my MOS to grunt." Wonder where this shit's leading?

"Hmm," he says, rubbing his chin intently and nodding his head. "Corporal Givens will be rotating home in a few weeks, and I'm going to need to break in a good man to take his place as company clerk. Think you might be interested in the job?"

A strange feeling comes over me, like a warm glow, and a ton of weight lifts off my shoulders. A veil of darkness falls from my heart and my eyes and for the first time since Beard died I feel a little bit alive again, and maybe there *is* reason to hope, maybe I *will* make it out of this place one day and go back to the World, the *real* World of peace and love and joy and beauty and no more killing and dying and hurt. . . . *Interested—are you shitting me, Top?* Does a bear shit in the woods? Does Chesty Puller have medals? Do Tijuana whores have sex? Interested? Damn right, I'm interested!

"Fucking-A, Top!" I blurt out before I realize what I'm saying. "I mean, yessir, Top, I'd like that I want it I think I can do a real good job for you, Top!" God, hope I haven't fucked it up.

He just laughs and says, fine, he'll be letting me know when he needs me. The CO dismisses me and I snap-to, shout "Aye, aye, Sir!" in my best militaristic bullshit voice, execute a smart about-face, and march out into the night, almost floating with euphoria.

Goodbye grunts and hello Remington Raiders! Teapot's my name, and REMF's my game. Just a couple of more weeks, then no more ground-pounding grunting for this dude's young ass. Skate City, here I come.

Something is wrong . . . very wrong. I can't put my finger on it, but I can feel it. A strong sense of foreboding, like something warning me to *"Stop!"* with every step I take. Like a silent voice of doom shouting for me not to go on, to make up some excuse—*any* excuse—just come up with some reason to sit this one out. Twist an ankle or break a leg or get a stomachache or faint or *something*— anything so you don't have to go on this one. But I tell the voice I can't, I *have* to go. Can't afford to fuck up now and jeopardize my chance for company clerk. Got a golden opportunity to spend the rest of my tour skating in the rear. Eight-month reward for just a couple of more weeks in Hell. Can't afford to pass that up—I *have* to go. No choice. Gotta do it.

We move on across the flats, waning moon glowing softly on the amber sand guiding our way. On and on, until the first rays of morning begin to turn the horizon pink, and the village stands in black silhouette before us.

Silently we spread out and take cover behind the scattered dunes and neglected, eroded dikes that separate the open flats from the vill awaiting quietly in the predawn shadows a hundred and fifty meters away. And we wait.

It dawns, and a light, erratic breeze rises and carries the odor of smoldering fires from yesterday's barrage to our nostrils. Overhead, the air sizzles and then whistles and the village erupts in a series of sharp explosions as our artillery begins to rain down upon the target. Round after round after round sending billowing gray-black mushrooms of earth and debris skyward until the vill is veiled in a cloud of destruction from which it seems nothing could escape and the air is heavy with the choking smell of cordite.

After what seems like hours, the barrage stops. The sun has cleared the treetops and burns a glaring path through the dissipating smog from what must've been hundreds of explosions. Sections of the vill becoming visible now against the clear sky as the winds increase and blow the veil away. The destruction is unbelievable. God, *nothing* could've lived through all that shit! Like a giant wrecking ball or a rampant tornado, the artillery has done its job.

Nothing seems untouched except for a grove of tall trees at the far end of the village. The once picturesque hamlet lies in ruins.

The company command group has positioned themselves directly behind our platoon, and Captain Langston is talking excitedly on the radio to battalion, chewing on his usual cigar. He gives the handset back to his RTO and says, to no one in particular, "We got 'em where we want 'em this time, youngsters!" grinning wide and pacing impatiently like a kid on Christmas morning who can't wait to get to the tree and tear open his presents.

The word is passed to move out. We spread out and get on-line. I force one foot to follow the other and try but fail to swallow the huge lump that always jumps to my throat. The vill looms a hundred meters away like an ominous monster getting ready to devour me but it's okay so far nothing yet maybe we'll be lucky maybe they've di-di'd or are all dead or. . . .

We get the word to fall back again, behind the last group of small dunes and dikes we just passed. I don't know what's up, and I don't care. This "fall back" stuff suits the shit out of me just fine. Maybe battalion changed its mind and we'll pass this one up, or maybe they think the pounding they gave it killed all the gooks so why bother or? . . .

Overhead, the air is seared again and a series of shells crash one after another amid the already devastated village. But they blow with a loud, hollow *poof!* rather than a thunderous explosion. What the fu—

Thin clouds of whitish smoke rise from the impact areas. That's not Willy Peter . . . Jesus, it's *CS!* Tear gas, and I don't even have my gas mask . . . shitcanned it like almost everybody else a long time ago . . . won't ever need it, they said, so there's no sense in humping it, is there? Way to go again, Mikey!

The mischievous wind carries wisps of the foul riot gas our way, and we bury our faces in our sleeves or towels and breathe as little and as shallowly as possible until the air clears. Then we're up and heading for the vill again, still dabbing at tearing eyes and trying to cough the burning from our throats.

Only seventy-five meters away now, and still nothing. Strangely quiet, a quiet that's almost too painful to bear. Piercing, foreboding silence that herald's the coming doom, like night follows day. Like the eye of a hurricane, I *know* it's out there somewhere waiting, waiting to spring up and snare me in that trap of terror that has grabbed me so many times before in its cruel, cold grip. My pulse races and my temples throb like the beating of tom-toms, and that nauseous chill runs through my bowels. For the first time since we got to the Cua Viet, I am fully alive and aware and the fear that had fled from me when Beard died has come back to haunt me with all its insidious might. I don't want to die here, not now. I want to live and be company clerk and go home and live to be a hundred and bounce great grandkids on my knobby knees. I have hopes and dreams and aspirations for the future and they don't include dying in this fucked-up godforsaken place on the far side of the world.

Fifty meters now. Maybe I'm worrying for nothing. The gooks have never let us get this close before . . . arty must've wiped 'em out. Yeah, or else they hauled ass during the night. Probably just gonna skate on through this vill, picking up the pieces and looking for souvenirs. Yeah, if it was gonna happen, the shit would've already hit the fa—

And then the whole world explodes!

A cacophony of orchestrated destruction surges up and blows from a thousand barrels like a volcano in violent eruption, engulfing us in its maddening roar. To my far right I see several Marines fall, and the dreaded strains of *"Corpsman up!"* is heard already amid the din of booming incoming and automatic weapons fire from the vill.

Most of our squad make it somehow to a row of small dunes on the left side of our broken lines. We crowd behind them, panting like winded horses, until Garcia, brows arched and eyes wild behind his fogging glasses, hollers, *"Let's go!"* and the squad is up and disappears around either end of the dunes toward the village. Except me. I can't move. . . . I try again, but the message from my brain to my legs has short-circuited and they refuse to work. Goddammit legs—*move!* There is no response. I stay cowered on my knees, listening to the already unbelievable noise of the battle growing louder and louder until individual sounds are swallowed up by the deafening raging waterfall. Oh god, god I'm scared never been so scared and I want to burrow deep into the sand like a gopher and hibernate until this awful blizzard of hot steel and death and madness is over but I can't I can't I can't let my buddies down gotta get up I gotta get up and go with 'em get up get up *goddammit get up!*

I fling myself around the left side of the dunes and sprint forward through the storm of lead for all I'm worth.

My world has become a hornets' nest as heavy automatic weapons' fire churns the ground all around me and hundreds of unseen stingers snap and pop and whine by me in deadly harmony. Running running so alive god I'm so alive never been so alive and alert to the sights and sounds and smells and every second might be my last so focus focus your eyes on something good that tree or dune or blue sky need to know the last thing you ever saw before you die think think of something pleasant from your life might be your last thought last thoughts oughta be good something nice something pleasant think of something good before you die. . . .

I spot Banks up ahead so I veer to the left and try to get on-line with him but the withering fire is merciless and the ground ahead of me is being stitched and erupting in sand geysers and it's all so unforgiving and I hurl myself desperately forward toward a slight depression that offers a tiny hope of survival from the blistering fire that seeks to cut me down.

27

Made it! I lift my head up slightly to look around, brushing the clinging sand from my face and spitting out the mouthful I nearly ate in my dive for safety. Ahead and a little to my right Banks hugs the earth, thirty or forty feet away. Well beyond his right I can see Garcia as he raises up ever so slightly and fires a round from his blooper at the vill. Near him I can barely make out the shoulders and helmet of another Marine. Larson, I think, or maybe Morton. Can't see anybody to my left . . . Jesus, there's nobody there. Me and Banks are it.

Trying to clear my head and gather my thoughts. Can't lift myself up high enough to aim and fire back. Got us pinned-down good. If me or Banks try to move we're dead meat. Gotta watch our flank, keep my eyes open on the flank.

The sharp *whistle-boom* of incoming artillery from across the DMZ continues to shower down on us, along with the *karrumph* of gook mortars from the vill, until the air seems saturated, filled beyond capacity and couldn't possibly hold any more but god oh god the hideous high-pitched *shriek-boom* of incoming rockets joins the circus of horrors with relentless fury, falling from the sky and tearing at flesh and bone and soul and sanity like a horde of screaming banshees.

Nowhere to go and nowhere to hide and we can't go forward and we can't go back and we can't dig in nothing to do but just lie here and take it and listen to the incoming and small-arms and automatic weapons and it's more than I ever imagined could happen been in the shit before lots of times and heavy shit too but not like this not like this oh god this is unreal a nightmare gotta be a nightmare can't be real *"Corpsman up!" "Corpsman!"* god they're hollering it from everywhere up and down the line not enough corpsmen in the company to handle this shit it's gotta stop it's gotta stop can't just lie here and take this anymore gotta do something.

Fuck it! I'm not gonna just lie here and die! I raise my rifle over the little rise of ground ahead of me and blindly squeeze the trigger. *Click.* Jammed! Useless son of a bitch is fucking jammed again! I lower the '16 to my face and check it out. Sand. Full of goddamn sand. How the hell are you supposed to keep the sand out? I fumble for my brush but can't find it, so I wipe at the grit with grimy fingers and the edge of my towel and blow. Eject the round and chamber another. Raise up to fire again, but a rocket screams and explodes just a few meters ahead, showering me with sand.

Jesus H. Christ! That was close! So alone . . . I feel so alone. I look over at Banks and scream out to him, "Hey Banks! Want me to come up there with you, man?"

He hollers back for me to stay where I am. I know he's right, of course, but I'm so scared and alone I want desperately to cling to somebody until this shit is over with or I wake up.

Another round screams in and explodes, closer still, kicking sand violently against me. I extract my face from the sand where I've buried it, wiping it from my eyes. I notice several tiny droplets of blood beading up and oozing from my left forearm. I stare at it, fascinated. For an instant I forget the awful noise and fear. I'm hit . . . son of a bitch. A purple heart. How about that shit. And then I'm snapped rudely back to the battle by the sight of a dozen or so NVA running to my left only seventy-five meters away and disappearing suddenly as though the earth just swallowed them up. God—they must be trying to flank us! I scream as loud as I can above the thunderous din, *"Banks! Gooks on the flank! Help me watch the flank!"* And then the world goes black. . . .

Faraway sensation of being lifted up and then slammed heavily to the ground . . . everything is black and gray like coal dust and the air is thick and hard to breathe . . . smells vaguely familiar, like the Fourth of July and firecrackers cherry bombs bottle rockets gunpowder . . . yeah, that's it, smells like gunpowder and the whole world is dark and fuzzy and buzzing and ringing and there's another smell too like something burning cloth or chicken or yeah that's it Daddy must be burning the chicken again. . . .

My head begins to clear, and then the pain—oh god the pain encompasses me tears through me rips me until I wish I could pass out or die . . . feels like a mule with a white-hot horseshoe kicked through my left rib cage. Anger merges with the pain. Goddamn, I'm gonna die, gonna fucking die and never see home or the beach or my family or friends again goddammit!

This is bad . . . this is bad . . . I'm hit hard. Never thought it would be like this. Never thought you could live with pain like this . . . hard to breathe, hard to breathe, can't get a good breath.

"Banks." The word comes out weakly, almost a whisper. I'm surprised and scared at the same time. I muster a breath and try again. *"Banks!"* Better this time. Think he heard me. Looking back this way. "I'm *hit* . . . hit bad!"

"Stay down . . . I'll be right there!" Fear in the voice, not so much from the ferocity of the battle probably as from the helplessness of what to do when he gets to me.

He doesn't come. He's pinned down and he can't come.

"Banks . . . I'm slipping . . . I'm slipping, man. . . . "

He screams for me to hold on, he'll be here in a minute, but still he doesn't come. Minutes pass like hours and the world continues to blow up all around us but it doesn't really matter to me anymore because I feel myself drifting away, drifting away and slipping into a warm dark tunnel and suddenly there is no more pain, only a warm and comforting buzzing and light vibration, and it's *so* peaceful and warm and calm and I'm drifting farther and farther into the void but it's safe in here I feel so safe and warm and secure and relaxed and quiet and peaceful . . . so peaceful . . . so serene. . . .

Far, far away, in some distant place that doesn't exist for me anymore, I hear my own unreal voice shouting at me and cursing me and telling me that I can always be dead but dead is forever and I better try to stay alive and live while I can. The voice is faint at first, barely perceptible, but it grows louder and louder and stronger and stronger and it's shouting in my ear now okay okay goddammit I'll fight I'm probably gonna fucking die anyway but right now I'm alive and there's a whole eternity to be dead for and god the pain the pain is back and the tunnel and the peaceful warmth is gone and the battle once again rages around me and the battle for my life rages within me.

Somehow Banks finally manages to crawl over to me. Checking me over, probably wondering what to do. I feel like my insides are all scrambled, so I ask him if my guts are hanging out.

He looks me over more closely. "No, you just got a big hole blown in your side."

His answer is strangely comforting, so I go on. "How about my toes? My legs and feet hurt bad, and I can smell my meat burning . . . are my toes gone?"

Scrutinizes me again. "They're all still there, I think. You got a big hunk of meat scooped off the top of your left foot, and a big hole in your left leg, and a bunch of smaller holes in both legs. But I think everything's still there."

Banks takes my battle dressing from the pouch on the back of my cartridge belt and places it gingerly over the hole in my side. Then he takes his own and ties it around the calf of my left leg. Tells me to hang on, he'll be right back, going after a corpsman, and then he's gone.

Nothing to do but lie here and wait and try to stay alive and listen to the sounds of this nightmare-come-true all around with the incessant booming and snapping and cracking and screaming—god, the screams! Half the company must be hit.

Don't know how long it's been, but Banks is back. Got Doc Andrews with him. I recognize Doc Andrews as one of the new guys from that other vill. Hell of an initiation. Also got PFC Jackson with him. Tall black dude from third squad. Third squad? Where the hell is everybody from our squad? Maybe this is it. Me and Banks. Only, I'm not so good anymore . . . weak, so damn weak. Can hardly talk, and it's hard to get a breath . . . gotta struggle to breathe . . . not much air, can't get much air. . . .

Doc says he can't give me morphine or anything for the pain because of the hole in my side. He's got all the bigger holes covered, so they untie my poncho from my belt, unroll it and as gently as possible lift me up and on it. Jackson looks down at me and smiles. Tells me I'm gonna be all right, they'll have me out of here in a minute. Banks and Doc each grab a corner of the poncho next to my head, and Jackson takes the rear. They lift me up and begin hauling me back toward the dunes in an ungainly trot like a three-legged horse. I'm swinging and bouncing and once or twice somebody stumbles and I hit the ground with a jolt and the pain wracks anew through my body but it's okay guys don't worry about it I just appreciate what you're doing for me.

Rounds are still rending the air with their awful hissing and cracking and kicking little sand geysers all around their feet but they trudge on through the maelstrom of fire like obedient beasts of burden toward the haven of the dunes. We're almost there when I feel a searing sensation across the cheeks of my ass as a round passes beneath me as close as you can get without cutting flesh. And then we're behind the dunes and Banks and Jackson and Doc are collapsed on hands and knees, gasping for breath.

Chaos reigns behind the dunes. We are protected from the swarms of small-arms fire that continue to snap and suck wind overhead, but the storm of incoming continues to pound dangerously close, angry whining shrapnel spinning malevolently through the air. Teams of corpsmen and grunts-turned-corpsmen work feverishly on the wounded who are piling up in alarming numbers. Some have managed to drag themselves back, but most are carried back by battle-weary grunts who somehow find the strength and courage for the painstakingly slow journey through the hell-storm. To one side, behind a low mound, are five or six Marines who no one bothers to attend . . . their war is over. At least three RTOs are talking excitedly on different nets, calling for medevacs or supporting fire.

Suddenly I can't breathe again, so I ask Banks and Doc Andrews to roll me over on my right side. They do as gently as possible, but it's worse now and after a few seconds I have them roll me onto my back again . . . don't know if I can hang on. . . .

A tall figure looms over me. I focus my eyes and recognize the First Sergeant. Worried look of almost fatherly concern across the wrinkled brow and deep-set eyes. He kneels beside me.

"Helms. How you doing?"

I think I manage a weak semblance of a smile through the pain and fear. "Okay, Top," I whisper, "I think I'll be okay." Sudden concern over job security flashes through my mind, and I add more strongly, "I still want that job when I get back, Top."

A big, warm smile crosses his face. "You got it, son. It'll be waiting for you." Pats me on the shoulder and moves on.

Trying to get a chopper in . . . big commotion going on all around. Can't see much for all the people moving around above me. Catch a glimpse of the chopper. Something's wrong . . . smoke puffing out, wobbling side to side . . . going down . . . oh Jesus, they've shot it down!

People all around me. Doc Poteat . . . hey, Doc. Checking me over again . . . I'm all right Doc, but I can't hardly breathe. Gonna get us out soon, he says. But how? Choppers can't get through. I see PFC Rice, our platoon RTO . . . not many others from our platoon. Banks is still around. There's Top . . . hope they get us out soon . . . so tired . . . weak . . . hard to believe so weak . . . can't even lift my arm up I'm so—

Shriek-boom! Oh god! Bodies falling all over me get off get off get 'em off what happened Jesus what happened? No no can't all be wounded oh please please god somebody help us please get us out of here!

The awful, choking dust clears and I see Top lying over on his side, all bloody and looking stunned but alive at least, and Banks is on his knees, bent over grimacing and clutching his torn arm or shoulder, blood pouring over his fingers and down his arm. Rice . . . oh god, look at Rice, lying on his back against a dune and blood is everywhere, not an inch where there's not blood, still holding the handset to his ear and telling someone we've got many more casualties than before and begging for medevacs. God, when is this shit gonna end? Can't die like this, not like this, get us out of here, they've gotta get us out of here.

I look up, and there's Larson squatting beside me, the flash suppressor of his M-14 glinting in the overhead sun. Must be helping to carry the wounded back . . . just like him to do that. We've drifted apart since Beard died . . . I want to reach up to him or smile or something, but I'm too tired and weak for even that now. My eyes . . . I try to tell him with my eyes. He looks through me, reaches down and squeezes my arm, and then he's gone. But he knows . . . he must know . . . he *has* to know!

It's been forever and still no letup from the pounding, but if the noise stopped now I think the silence would kill us all. Somebody's picking me up and I'm swaying and bouncing again, then everything grows dark and hollow. I smell diesel fuel and hear the rumbling of an engine. I strain to look around. Wounded everywhere, stacked shoulder to shoulder, moans and crying, somebody keeps screaming . . . shut up make him shut up goddammit if I could move I'd make him shut up.

Moving and jolting. Familiar growling noise . . . all hollow . . . amtrack . . . we're on an amtrack . . . not on but in . . . inside the amtrack and leaving the noise and the terror behind but another terror in here all dark and they keep crying and screaming why don't they shut up it's safe now safe in here can't shoot down an amtrack but . . . mines . . . could hit a mine oh god please please don't let us hit a mine.

Bright light again. Being carried. Wind whipping my face stinging my face I squeeze my eyes against the wind and sand and I'm laid down hard in the chopper several piled next to me and Banks is there sitting up against the side his arm all bandaged and blood seeping through and the noise grows and the chopper shakes and shakes and the vibration rumbles through my body and jars my pain and we're up and tilting sharply hope I don't slide out god don't let me fall out!

Flying away now. Away from the awful sounds and smells and fear and horror. Away from the war.

28

"Doc, I think I'm gonna throw up." My whispered warning is barely audible above the humming activity inside the big triage room at Delta Med. Hollow-eyed, overworked corpsman looks up from the foot of the table I'm lying on. Finishes pushing the catheter tube up into my bladder and lays the bag between my knees.

"Just turn your head and puke on the floor so you don't choke."

I turn my cheek against the cool table and heave blackish-brown vomit over the side onto the deck. All around me rows and rows of tables are filled with wounded grunts, and the aisles are a highway of rushing corpsmen and nurses. Even in my pain I feel a wave of embarrassment wash over me as I lie naked and helpless. Against a far wall several bodies lie unmoving in ghastly silence. Some are covered with sheets or ponchos, but others stare with that death-gaze toward the cold ceiling. Except for the one without a face who has lost even that small dignity.

I turn away, back to the corpsman as he affixes another IV bottle to the stand above my table. Adjusts the flow and asks me my name and age and where I'm from and a dozen other bullshit questions again. Trying to keep me from going into shock, I guess. Turns to another corpsman holding a clipboard and pencil and tells him I'm to go on the first flight out to Phu Bai.

Being wheeled on a gurney down a brightly lit corridor. I'm so tired I can hardly keep my eyes open, but I'm scared and I have to know what's going on with me.

Don't remember much about the flight down from Dong Ha. C-130, I think, but not sure.

Walls are white and it looks like a hospital back in the World would look. . . . Nurses and corpsmen and other personnel busy walking by. I'm so tired.

Someone standing over me now, telling me I'll be going into surgery soon but first they need some x-rays. Dressed in pale blue . . . funny-looking cap on his head. Must be a doctor.

Oh god, they're torturing me, moving me around and twisting me in all kinds of positions, telling me to "breathe" and "hold it" and "got to do it again, you moved" but I didn't move I just fell over Doc I'm too damn weak to move I fell not gonna need surgery they're gonna fucking kill me here.

Bright round lights overhead so bright and pretty eyes staring at me from over the mask must be a nurse more eyes and masks and caps the tall one tells me to just relax the shot will make me sleep just breathe and relax breathe and relax so bright the lights are so bright pain is fading starting to get sleepy just let go and be sleepy and relax getting darker now faint and fuzzy and relax and sleep getting so sleepy so sl—

Sluurrp . . . gurgle gurgle . . . sluurrp . . . gurgle gurgle . . . sluurrp . . . gurgle gurgle . . . Somebody keeps sucking on that damn straw. *Sluurrp . . . gurgle gurgle . . . sluurrp . . . gurgle gurgle . . .* Over and over and over, like kids slurping their sodas at the Saturday matinee. Wish they'd finish. Starting to bother me and wake me up. *Sluurrp . . . gurgle gurgle . . .* Surrounded by that irritating noise. Gonna shove them straws up somebody's ass in a minute.

My eyes flutter open and blink at the darkness which turns to dim gray as they slowly adjust. Blurred blue wall rises up and merges with white tiled ceiling. Hundreds of tiny holes dance back and forth and up and down across the ceiling, playing games with my tired eyes. My gaze slides down the wall and bounces off the foot of the sheeted bed, focusing on the two peaks that rise above the snow-swept plain. I wiggle my toes and the summits move, but the pain jolts through me and I am rudely reminded that I'm wounded and in a hospital.

Low, constant humming, like an aquarium pump, provides background music as the slurping and gurgling continues around me. Trying to clear the cobwebs from my mind. Remembering now . . . the vill . . . couldn't take the vill . . . tried but got pinned down . . . bad shit. Gonna be company clerk but got hit. . . . somebody else'll probably get it now. . . . Top said he'd hold it for me but he got hit too . . . bad shit . . . seems like everybody got hit . . . hurt bad . . . pain, god the pain . . . not so bad now, if I don't move . . . sore though . . . sore to breathe, but not bad pain.

Sluurrp . . . gurgle gurgle . . . Jesus H. Christ! Had it with that shit. Gonna tell 'em to knock it off! I turn my head to the left. Through the shadows I can make out a bed with the upper end elevated at about a forty-five degree angle. Bare chest and shoulders and neck rise above the covering sheet, but there's no head. Jesus, no head! But then my eyes focus better and I see the head is swathed in gauze dressing that blends perfectly into the sunken pillow. Looks like a fresh Egyptian mummy. On the side, near the front of the wrapped head, a dark stain surrounds a tube that runs from the mouth to the source of my irritation. Like a dripping faucet in the middle of the night, the pump of the suction machine kicks on and off, on and off, over and over, draining blood and saliva from the head before it can leak down the throat and into the lungs and drown the mummy.

The sight changes the sound from irritating to horrifying and I turn my head away to escape it but oh god there's another one on my other side slurping and gurgling louder and louder and Jesus why do I have to be here between twin mummies and their blood-sucking machines why don't they get them out of here away from me I can't stand it much longer gonna go fucking crazy if it keeps on much longer.

A corpsman materializes suddenly beside my bed. He pulls the sheet from my shoulders and sticks a thermometer in my armpit. I want to ask him why he's doing it that way but my mouth is so dry I need to swallow first and find some moisture so I strain to swallow and oh Jesus something's in my throat I can feel something down my throat and I struggle for all I'm worth to bring my left hand up and there's a tube coming out of my nose and I follow it wild-eyed across the pillow and off the bed and over to my own personal horrible suction machine.

The doc tells me to calm down, I'm doing fine and will be all right. Straightens out the IV tubes I kinked up in my frantic groping, holds my wrist and stares at his watch. Wraps a wide black band around my bicep and pumps it up, then releases the pressure while he listens to my arm with a stethoscope. So damn methodical.

Then the corpsman peels away the large bandage that's covering my abdomen. I glance down and recoil at what I see—a long, puckered row of skin running from my breastbone to my pubic bone, like some hideous ridge line, held together with wire sutures. He removes two smaller bandages on either side of my stomach, revealing large flat oval tubes, three or four inches long. Oh god! Scared shitless now.

"Doc . . . is that my intestines?" Weak, croaking inquiry.

He chuckles. "No, Marine. That's just a couple of drainage tubes. Routine for your type of surgery. Won't be in there but a few days. Take it easy. You're doing fine."

Changes the bandages, swabs my arm with a cotton ball and jabs me with a needle. Tells me to rest now, he'll check on me later. Then he's gone.

Slurping and gurgling growing fainter now. No longer scary. Pain and discomfort and fear disappearing behind the cloud of euphoria I'm floating on. Feel real good, so relaxed and pleasant and tired, but good kind of tired . . . safe now . . . can sleep here . . . no gooks . . . no war . . . just close my eyes and drift away.

Awake again, but I'm not in the dark room with the blue walls and the mummies. Bright in here, lots of windows. I close my eyes to shut out the brightness but it passes through the lids and hurts my eyes anyway.

A corpsman passes by and I catch his attention with a feeble wave of my hand. I whisper that the light hurts my eyes and I want to go back to my dark room now. He gives me a funny look and tells me there is no "dark room," that I'm in Danang and that I've been here for two days now. Asks me if I need anything for pain.

Danang? Thought I was in Phu Bai. . . . Yeah, Doc, sure. I'm hurting bad. Gimme something for the pain. I nod my head and the corpsman disappears.

Danang? How did I get here? Don't remember shit. I try to look around but the light is still painful. I peer through squinted eyes and make out a long row of beds occupied with resting or groaning patients. A whole world of hurting grunts.

The corpsman returns. I ask him how long before I get back to the bush. He looks down at me like I'm crazy and tells me I'm going to Japan this afternoon or tomorrow morning. *Swab-jab-swab.* Floating away again.

Conscious again but not sure if this is today or tomorrow. Swaying with a slight jolting rhythm. Open my eyes and see I'm being carried on a stretcher up a ramp. Bright sky disappears and the glare is swallowed up by the dark cave we enter. My bearers slide my stretcher onto the bottom rack of the stacked stanchions which line both sides of the C-130. Hectic activity and clouded mumbled conversations fill the cargo bay of the aircraft. Everything is foggy and muffled though I can feel the vibration of the warming engines as the loading continues.

One of the patients above me goes into violent convulsions and a team of corpsmen and nurses rush to his aid. Somebody knocks my IV bottle off its hook and it shatters in a thousand pieces upon the metal deck. The poor bastard dies and they off-load him. My IV tube dangles on the deck and fear grabs me that I'll die too without it. I holler with all my being, but it comes out a weakly whispered "Doc . . . Doc" as corpsman after corpsman passes by me, not noticing my desperate plight.

I am amazed and saddened at my utter weakness and helplessness. I am worse off than a newborn infant. Infants can at least fill their lungs with air and inundate the nursery with their crying needs. I can do nothing.

Somehow I manage to lift my left arm off the stretcher and let it fall over the side, dangling. An angel of mercy finally notices what has happened. The beautiful face lowers close to mine and smiles sweetly, assuring me that everything is okay and they'll fix me right up. Too weak to even smile back as the olive-drab Florence Nightingale disappears up the aisle.

A minute later and I'm being hooked up to another bottle. Engines growing louder as we begin to taxi. Everything is hazy . . . fading away.

Lying in my rack, staring at the ceiling, waiting for my pain and sleep meds. Been here at Yokosuka Naval Hospital in Japan for almost two weeks now. Been in and out of consciousness most of that time, so I don't remember much of what's going on. Last couple of days are about all I can really recall.

During his rounds this morning, Doctor Forrest looked me over and told the nurse and corpsman with him that I was ready to start getting up. Also said it was time for my catheter to come out. I was glad to get rid of that piss bag, but I almost died from embarrassment when the nurse pulled back the sheet, grabbed my shriveled member with one hand and pulled the tube out with the other. Jesus. You'd think she'd let the corpsman do it! At least it was Major Pennington. She's probably around forty years old. Sort of the grand-motherly type. Glad it wasn't that good-looking lieutenant who pulls the night shift. She's enough to give anybody a good case of the blue balls. No telling what might've happened if she would've performed that delicate procedure. In my condition, probably nothing. Wishful thinking.

After the tube came out the corpsman raised my bed, put his arm under my back and lifted me upright, while Major Pennington supported my shoulder so I wouldn't fall over. God, did it hurt! So damn sore, all over. Dizzy as hell, like I'd been on a good drunk. Felt like I'd been run over by a convoy of six-bys. Hurt City.

After a while the room quit spinning and I was able to sit up by myself for a few minutes. They eased me back down and said we'd do better next time. Did that shit four times today, and it hurt like hell every time. Good to be off my back, though. Supposed to try to stand tomorrow. On what? Both feet and legs feel shot to shit. I can hardly wait.

* * *

Made me stand up this morning and take a couple of steps. Sat me up on the edge of the bed for a few minutes, then two corpsmen supported my arms and eased me to the floor. When my weight settled on my legs and feet I almost passed out from the searing pain that shot through me like a white flash. I would've fell flat on my face if they hadn't caught me. Jesus H. Christ, it hurt! I told them no thanks, I'd rather be an invalid, but they said to quit bitching, that there's a lot of guys a whole lot worse off than me, and besides I gotta do it anyway, doctor's orders. Asshole fucking swabbies pissed me off! Wasn't about to let no squids think I was a pussy, so I struggled through five or six agonizing steps down the aisle with one of the docs supporting me in case I fell on my ass, and the other trailing alongside, rolling my rack of IV bottles. Just about the worst hump I ever took, but I made it.

God, I feel bad . . . chest hurts . . . all tight and I can't breathe good. Dark in here. Why don't they turn on the lights? Where am I anyway? All wet . . . all wet here . . . so hot and wet and dark.

Drip . . . drip . . . drip . . . faucet's on . . . somebody left the faucet on and it's dripping and dripping turn it off somebody please turn it the fuck off it's wetting me and I'm all hot and dark and wet please turn it off so I can get cool and dry.

A corpsman makes his rounds and I try to call out to him to find out why I'm all wet. He hears me and walks over. He slips and nearly falls next to my bed. Shines his flashlight and rushes away.

Pretty night nurse and two corpsmen around my bed. Light is on now so I look to see what I'm lying in. Mostly clear fluid, spotted by brownish-red blood oozing from the wound in my side, soaking the mattress and dripping into a puddle on the floor. Still having trouble breathing . . . shallow efforts at best. The pretty face barks orders and the two docs hurry away. She places a thermometer under my tongue and follows after them.

As soon as her back is turned I pull the thermometer from my mouth and squint to focus and read it. One-oh-four and rising. Oh Jesus . . . now I know where they've gone. The ice . . . god, I'm going back in the ice again.

29

Not sure how much time has passed, but I'm a lot better now. Getting stronger every day, and don't feel nearly so sick. Able to breathe a lot easier, too. Got another tube running through the big hole in my ribcage into my lung. Hooked up to the suction machine again, but I'm used to it by now. No big deal.

This afternoon one of the corpsmen said he had a surprise for me. Clamped my drainage tube with a hemostat and unhooked me from the suction machine. Helped me get out of bed and stand up. I asked him what was going on. He said it was time I started using the head. Held up a package for me to see and smiled sadistically. An enema. Oh, shit.

Hobbled down the aisle to the head, the doc and my IVs close behind. Doc followed me into a stall and positioned the stand holding my IVs next to the toilet. Tore open the package and read me the instructions. Asked me if I wanted any help, still grinning like a bear in a bee tree. I told him to fuck off, that I could shove it up my ass all by myself, thank you. Held it as long as I could, then let it fly. First crap I've taken since I got here over three weeks ago. Felt ten pounds lighter. Doc checked the results and said I did real good. Jesus, felt like a damn toddler being praised for potty training.

Took me into surgery this morning to close the big wound in my left calf. Shrapnel blew a big chunk of muscle out, about the size of a tennis ball. Too big to close by itself, so they cut more flesh away and elongated the wound into the shape of a football, then squeezed it together and stitched it up. They only gave me a local, so I got to watch them work on me, looking through a mirror. Really weird to lie there and watch somebody snip away at my body, but I was so doped up on Demorol anyway that it was almost funny. Lying there, cracking jokes with the corpsmen while they cut a little hunk here and a little there, throwing bloody meat and gauze into a pan beside the table. Fascinating.

They haven't decided what to do about the scooped-out wound on top of my left foot yet. The doctor said they may have to graft skin later, but for now they're just going to keep it clean and see if it heals over by itself. Tendons and ligaments and little whitish-looking nodules are clearly visible. Kinda grosses me out to watch them change the dressings on that one.

The wounds on my other leg are doing okay. My ankle's still swollen pretty bad where the bone was chipped, but the holes don't look too bad and I can hobble around the ward on my own now. Just clamp my tube with a hemostat, unhook the drain, and hump around using my IV stand for a crutch. Nothing to it. I'll be running a four-minute mile soon, the way I'm going. The docs were right. A lot of guys are much worse off than I am. Little spic dude from rockets in our weapons platoon is *all* fucked up. Seen him all stretched out, cut from chest to crotch like me, but they've got his incision spread open wide with all kinds of tubes running everywhere. He looks like shit. Got a feeling he ain't gonna make it.

Another dude from our first platoon got moved off our ward to ICU yesterday. I remember him being shot through the forearm near Con Thien back in December, just a flesh wound. He was sitting there, grinning with pride about his purple heart and all that shit guys tend to do when they get a skating wound. He got hit real bad on the Cua Viet. Nothing to smile about with this one. I figure he's gonna buy it for sure, because his parents flew here from the World to see him, one of the docs told me.

Then there's the guy from another ward with the face. Saw him in the hallway yesterday. Christ. Lips and nose mostly gone, the face contorted horribly into an ugly road map of massive, reddish scars. Doc Smallwood told me he's requested to go back to Nam instead of the World. I don't blame him. Looks worse than the Phantom of the Opera. If I was him I'd want to go back and die too.

Hobbling down the aisle to the back of the ward, heading for the whirlpool where I'll sit for half an hour or so in the swirling warm water as it debrides and cleans my wounds. I like these treatments. Garbled strains of "Respect" tormenting my ears for the millionth time as a group of recuperating splibs gather around, jiving to the battery-weakened sounds of Aretha Franklin. Jesus H.

Christ! That shit irritates me more than my wounds—over and over and over, twenty-four hours a day it seems. If I had the strength I'd shove that tape recorder right up their ass. Or buy 'em some new batteries or a different tape or something. Anything to stop that god awful screeching racket. Makes Morton sound like Bing Crosby.

I pass by the small rec room that borders the therapy room. Look at *that* shit! Reruns of *Bonanza* playing on the small black and white television set. The Cartwrights ride up to the porch of their ranch house and dismount. Pa speaks sternly to the boys in rapid-fire Japanese. Big ol' Hoss takes his ten-gallon hat off his head, looks around sheepishly, shifting the weight of his massive frame from one foot to the other. Answers Pa in a high-pitched jabbering of at least a thousand words-per-minute rate of fire, while on the screen his mouth barely moves. The handful of ailing Marines seated in the rec room howl with laughter, and I can't help but join them as the pain shakes through my body.

Just got finished with my supper of some soft, mushy glob of shit. Oh well, beats feasting from an IV bottle, I guess. Propped up in my rack, reading the latest issue of *Stars and Stripes*.

How about that shit! LBJ says he ain't gonna run again. Good. Maybe we'll get a president who'll have the balls to let us go all out and end this damn war. . . .

Jesus! Somebody zapped Martin Luther King, and now all the black dudes are on a rampage, rioting and burning and tearing the cities apart. Looting and shooting . . . christ, what the fuck's happening back in the World?

Casualty list . . . almost afraid to look, but I can't stop

myself. . . . Jesus, this is bad. Looks like a who's who list
for Two-Four. . . . Oh, shit! *Hubbard!* The big, gentle giant
from first squad. Chilling, icy shivers dance up my spine as
I read on. . . . *Kantz!* Oh Jesus, they got Kantz! Damn, he
was so short. He should've already been out of the bush. I
close my eyes and recall the scene of him waving at me
and Larson as first platoon moved out ahead of us to
assault another vill on the Cua Viet. Red hair and round,
freckled face standing out so clearly against the blue sky.
"Eight days and a wake up!" he'd hollered at us. "Just eight
more days and a wake up and it's back to the Land of the
Big PX for me!" But now he's dead, and the only place he's
going to is the land of body bags and silver coffins and row
upon row of bronze markers and white crosses. Goddamn—he should've been out of the bush by then. Why
the fuck didn't they get him out of the bush?

Scared now. Really scared. *"Don't go on!"* my mind
screams to my eyes, but they are compelled to disobey and
continue down the list, skipping unrecognized names and
pausing briefly on those I think I know . . . far too many.
Forced on by some strange and senseless power, down,
down the morbid black-on-white rows of America's latest
harvest of death. Straining hard now against the irre-
sistible, unseen, merciless entity that drags my unwilling
eyes across the jagged letters, tears welling and starting to
flow, down, down past the Ks to the Ls and *no! Don't keep
going* stop stop it or you know what will happen oh god—
you *know* it's going to be there you can feel it you know
you know! . . .

Larson, Jack P., LCpl, E Co. 2nd Bn 4th Marines . . .

Oh, god! The muted scream dies in my throat, and I

grow cold and go limp, and the only strength left in my body allows the tears to flow down my cheeks in silent, sobbing torrents as my useless arms flop helplessly to my sides and the paper falls, fluttering to the floor.

Phone call from home. I can't believe this shit. I should feel joy or happiness or something good inside, knowing my family is waiting to talk to me from back in the World. But I just feel empty. Empty and bothered. I don't want to talk. What am I going to say? I have nothing *to* say. I don't know them anymore. How do I explain to those people that the son and brother they seek is no more? That he ceased to be back there somewhere along the way, and that someone else, someone they don't even know, now exists within this shattered, wasted shell. How do I explain?

30

To every thing there is a season, and a time to every purpose under the heaven:
A time of war, and a time of peace . . .
A time to kill, and a time to heal. . . .

—Ecclesiastes

I'm going home. Back to the World. Doctor Forrest gave me the word this morning during his rounds. It's hard to explain what I feel right now. Relief? Joy? Sadness? I don't know. A mixture, I guess.

When he first gave me the news it felt like a thousand pounds had been lifted off my shoulders. That underlying fear of going back to the bush that had been gnawing away at me vanished, like someone flipped a switch and turned on the lights and chased the dark away. After so much death and destruction and killing and suffering I never really thought I'd make it home. I almost cried.

But there's another side, too. Been lying here, thinking about the last six months and all that's happened. About

Beard and Larson and so many others. All those plans and hopes and dreams that will never be. Shot to shit. Somehow it just doesn't seem right. I'm going home and they're dead—forever. It's not fair, goddammit, it's just not *fair!* I feel like I cheated them. I'm glad I'm alive, I'm glad I didn't die over there, but they didn't deserve to fucking die either.

I cover my burning eyes with clenched fists and try to make the hurt go away, but it won't. It's like a cancer, eating away at my very soul . . . never gonna go away . . . always gonna be there.

What about the guys still back in the bush? I'm going home and they're still gonna be there, humping and suffering and fighting and killing and dying—Jesus, I feel like a goddamn deserter. Part of me wants to be back there with them, and part of me wants to go home and forget forever. I guess I did my part, but they did theirs too, and they're still doing it. I'm going home, and some of them never will. I feel like I should be there with them, but I'm glad I'm not. Christ, how am I supposed to live with *that?*

And Thompson, poor Thompson. A moment of craziness and his life is fucked up forever. Probably gonna do hard time, but even if he beats it he's got to live forever with what he did. Christ, how can a person live with *that* horror? Not even his fault, really. He didn't mean it. Oh, he pulled the trigger, all right, but he didn't kill Beard. No this fucking *war* killed Beard. I think maybe this war has killed us all.

I ease painfully out of bed and shuffle the few feet across the floor to the window. Still afraid to be exposed in the open, so I stand to one side and peer out. The hospital grounds are awash with evidence of the early spring.

Tender blades of green are beginning to dot the past winter's carpet of amber-brown. The cherry trees are crowned in all their glory, and the pink and white arbor shimmers delicately in the light breeze. A snow-white cloud drifts lazily across the most beautiful blue sky I can remember.

A colorful little bird alights atop a budding rosebush and throws his head back in trilling song to herald the passing of one season to another. The long harsh winter is over, and the earth has begun to renew itself.

The scene outside is a stark contrast to the bleakness of broken bodies and wasted youth I see inside these walls as I quickly glance around the ward. I turn from the suffering within and concentrate again on the beauty without.

Suddenly the songster is joined by his mate, nesting material hanging out both sides of her tiny beak. They take wing together, and I watch as they disappear into the maze of pink petals of a nearby tree. A smile crosses my heart. I am going home. It is time to heal.

DON'T FORGET TO LOOK FOR THESE EXCITING REAL-LIFE WAR STORIES...

Band of Brothers by Stephen E. Ambrose
0-7434-6411-7 / $7.99 U.S. / $11.99 Can.

The Do-Or-Die Men by George W. Smith
0-7434-7005-2 / $6.99 U.S. / $10.50 Can.

Hill 488 by Ray Hildreth and Charles W. Sasser
0-7434-6643-8 / $6.99 U.S. / $10.50 Can.

Bloody Ridge by Michael S. Smith
0-7434-6321-8 / $6.99 U.S. / $10.50 Can.

Reflections of a Warrior by Franklin D. Miller
with Elwood J.C. Kureth
0-7434-6499-0 / $6.99 U.S. / $10.50 Can.

AVAILABLE FROM POCKET BOOKS

POCKET BOOKS
A Division of Simon & Schuster
A VIACOM COMPANY

09605

Visit
❖ **Pocket Books** ❖
online at

....

www.SimonSays.com

....

Keep up on the latest new
releases from your favorite
authors, as well as author
appearances, news, chats,
special offers and more.

SIMON & SCHUSTER
A VIACOM COMPANY
www.SimonSays.com

Pocket
Books

2381-01